Retail Store Leadership

Graham R Little PhD AFNZIM

2000

First published in 2000 by Management Books 2000 Ltd
Cowcombe House
Cowcombe Hill
Chalford
Gloucestershire GL6 8HP
Tel. 01285 760 722
Fax. 01285 760 708
E-mail: mb2000@compuserve.com

Printed and bound in Great Britain by Biddles, Guildford

British Library Cataloguing in Publication Data is available
ISBN 1-85252-338-7

Contents

Contents

Preface

Welcome. You are one of the exceptional people of the world who actually read the preface. In reading this book and acting on the ideas in it, you will be taking steps to fulfilling your potential as a manager and fulfilling some of the goals and aims that have shaped what I have done for thirty years. I gain much fulfilment and quiet satisfaction from seeing and knowing that people have gained, grown and developed from things I have done with them and said to them.

This book is one of a series, with several yet to come. I have for many years been primarily involved in doing a lot for a few, through personal and direct involvement with people. This series is a concerted effort to bring my thought to a wider, indirect audience. I think that several points of philosophy make my thought different. I dislike fads, always have. So I have sought timelessness in the works – things a manager should be doing now, and still be doing in years to come. So this series is not intended to be the 'latest fad', nor the flavour of the month in management thinking. Business is a long-term, highly repetitious activity, frequently requiring people to do the same thing today, tomorrow and the next day and next. So I try to ensure my work is based on the 'reality bites', the simple, disciplined things that have to be done and done again. I also believe that management is often made overly complicated in a conceptual sense. In my experience, the really hard part is living out the things that, as a manager, one knows should be lived out, rather akin to Daniel Goleman's emotional intelligence. If in addition to the demands on the will, the spirit and self-discipline, the concept is also complicated, then the request on the manager is becoming nigh impossible. So I have sought simple concepts, focusing emphasis on living them out.

The books are based on my personal experience. Most of this has been good, but I have also lost a company and lost a lot of money, which was not good. I learned, and this has added another dimension to my thinking and my work. I did not know it at the time, but looking back, I lived as I did as a process of gaining experience. Frequently I could have chosen safer paths and secure options. I did not, and if I had, then I could never have written this work in this way. Like a good novelist who researches the people and their place, so I did my research, real time.

The first few books, five in all, consist of one completely new concept, *The Five Steps to Better Business Leadership* and four books based on earlier works. These latter four have been updated and strengthened from my experience and development of my thinking since they were first written. They have a harder 'edge'. Three of the books *Sales Team Leadership, Operations Team Leadership* and *Retail Team Leadership* have the same introduction. This is done for the reason that the great majority of managers will buy only one of these – they are either in sales, operations or retail, and unlikely to be in two at any one time.

So what should a manager read of this series? A full development program would cover the books *The Five Steps of Business Leadership Success, Management Team Leadership* and one of *Sales, Operations* or *Retail Leadership*. They all offer different things each from a different point of view. Three books is a lot in one sitting, so reading them and working through them could take quite some time. It is important that not only do you read, but also think about how to act on what you read and where and how the ideas can be applied in your business and team. If you want a better result, then you need to act differently from how you acted yesterday. These books will guide you on what to do and how to do it. They can help with more will, but mostly they describe how to achieve greater skill.

Forthcoming books concern motivation, training, leadership and the will to win. The first two directly continue the work begun in the first five books. The other two are more general, somewhat focused on more personal development issues – issues, can I say, that are more spiritual (in a totally non-religious sense). This goes to the heart of my experience of good leaders – almost inevitably they were hard on the outside, committed to the success of their enterprise, doing what had to be done. But these leaders were soft on the inside, their humanity and sensitivity evident under their self-discipline, and offering something beyond today's pound. They were people to whom one could and did relate, but they also filled others with confidence that the enterprise would thrive under their leadership and that you as a person would always be given careful thought if ever there were problems needing hard decisions.

So I entrust you to my work, and hope for you the very best you are able to be.

Graham Little, Auckland, NZ, April 2000

Introduction

Getting a better result

This book series focuses on the thinking and behaviour of the management team and key staff. It improves operating profit by altering the focus, and the actions of these staff are changed in the direction of improved operating profit.

There are four books in the series, **Management Team Leadership**, **Sales Team leadership**, **Operations Team Leadership** and **Retail Store Leadership**. A fifth book, **The Five Steps To Business Leadership Success** provides the overview for all of the four 'leadership' books and offers an analysis of a simple yet extremely practical theory of management and organisation that leads to simple yet effective guidelines on how to act as a business leader to get the best possible results from a team.

If you believe there is potential to improve the performance of yourself your team and your business, then this book series will assist you to achieve that result.

Business Momentum

Think of a business as a flywheel – once going, it is not hard to keep it going in the same direction at the same speed. But it is very hard to increase speed or change direction. The momentum of a business lies in the behaviour and thinking of the staff and in the behaviour and thinking of the customers and potential customers.

Maintaining the momentum of a business is not difficult. To increase that momentum requires the injection of focused effort. This energy that is needed to increase the momentum can and must come from the management team and key staff. This 'extra effort', that is the effort to increase the momentum of a business, I call the *'creative input'* by the team. I define creativity in business as that effort that increases the momentum of a business to greater, permanent increases in operating profit or market share or return on funds employed, or whatever factor is selected by the senior management.

What this book can do for you

If you picked up this book, then obviously you were looking for something. Somewhere, conscious or not, there is a quest within you. Perhaps it is to better yourself, perhaps to get a better result from your team or business, or perhaps, like I have been at times in my life, you are looking for something without knowing you are looking and without knowing what it is you are looking for.

Let me tell you something about this book series. It can do four things for someone willing to think about what it has to say and who has at least a little of the questing in them.

✓ The books can strengthen the attitude of striving and self-belief on which all success must ultimately rest. They can and will move you forward toward the best possible for you. Thus the books can facilitate emotional skills.

✓ Importantly, the books explore many important concepts and conceptual structures. We are predominantly a thinking species. The more effectively we think about situations, the more effective we are likely to act toward that situation. The books can and will develop conceptual skills.

✓ An important philosophy developed throughout the books is that business is only rational in retrospect. Fundamentally, the forward momentum of a business is emotional, and the crucial forward direction, often day by day, is created. By exploring how to improve insight and identify opportunity, the books develop creative skills.

✓ Finally, much of the books are devoted to implementing the ideas and opportunities that emerge. Repeatedly I find that the best businesses are those with every day creative talent who can and do implement with care and precision the ideas before them. Often those ideas are simple, even basic. Seldom are the ideas very clever. The books will develop your skills at making real the sharp effective ideas that can increase the operating profit in your business.

How to best use the books

There are three necessary factors needed for effective action: knowing what to do, knowing how to do it and having the will to get it done. Having picked up the book, there is some sense of quest in you that is all that is needed to begin. It is a myth that we must be motivated and inspired to achieve. Think of mowing the lawns or doing some other chore that you do not think is rewarding but must be done. Often I find with such chores that once I get started I find it is not so bad, and at the end I look back and think, 'well that's a good job done, it wasn't bad, I almost enjoyed it'. What it took to get me going was the disciplined kick-start. Once I got going, I became more motivated. I think this is general – motivation follows action, not the other way around.

The introduction provides the guide to what to do to improve the bottom line of your business. It is based on the idea of profit profile developed by John Tracy in his book *Profit Dynamics* (Ref 17). It is a simple yet very effective tool for assessing the key factors that influence operating profit and for exploring how to manipulate those factors to increase operating profit. Having established what, the books then consider how and build the will to keep at it.

Goal focused

The technique is very goal-focused because the process I adopt is based on the proposition that for every goal there are behaviours that must be acted out if the goal is to be achieved. And this applies to all goals, whether in sports, business, and life generally. I call this the **goal←→action** principle and also the **fundamental principle of organisation** (see *The Five Steps to Successful Business Leadership*).

The development of professional conduct is thus to make the goals clear, then to identify the behaviours most likely to facilitate the goals, and finally, to review with the people whether or not they are acting out the behaviours with the level of commitment needed to achieve the result. For example, if you wanted to be an internationally competitive swimmer, then you need to spend a great deal of time in a swimming pool with due commitment. Going through the motions simply won't cut it, in sport or business.

Personal development and the importance of challenge

Too often training and development is conducted in a passive environment where the urgency to change is low. Consider for a moment when a person loses a close family member. It is quite typical for that person afterwards to say how they feel they have grown, and how they are now able to cope with more than they could before the tragic loss. The growth is a result of the struggle to cope, to get through the days doing what must be done, and the discipline to manage one's emotions and urges, not to give in.

The same principle applies to developing greater leadership and refining the professional conduct in a business. It is refining the focus on 'doing what must be done', rather than 'doing what I feel like' or 'doing just enough'. I can guarantee one thing, that if you invest in these ideas, if you take a non-passive approach to your own development as a leader, if you challenge yourself, then the investment will be repaid. You are worthy of investing in yourself, but you must challenge yourself in terms of your thinking and the disciplined nature of your actions.

Offering a challenge to business teams

The principle of a challenge to facilitate growth is applied to business teams through a process of presenting to the team a *'creative statement'*. This is a statement from the team leader requesting greater performance from the team and specifying the level of improvement he or she expects.

Thus the starting point for facilitating improved management in your business is the question: *is there any aspect of business performance that you would like to see improved and by how much?*

This becomes the creative challenge for the team. We need to do the same with ourselves, that is to challenge our own performance, raise our own expectations of ourselves, not to the point of being impossible but to the point where it stretches us. In the striving to achieve, we grow as people and as business leaders.

Improvements at the edge

Most businesses are well run. If there were something obvious to do that would improve performance, it would have been done. Also, I find that in most businesses, the people do things 80% effectively 80% of the time. But what would benefit the business is to have them doing things 90% effective 90% of the time. This I call improvement at the edge. The effort required is exponential, that is going from 80:80 to 90:90 is as hard as getting to 80:80 in the first place.

Perhaps, above all else it is this philosophy of striving, the clear cut attitude exhibited in behaviour that we can always do better that makes the crucial difference between the average team and the great team. It follows that the ability to instil this attitude into a team is what makes the difference between the average leader and the great leader.

Team Leader as coach

For the book series to succeed for you, you must commit yourself to improved performance. Once you are committed, and if you are a team leader, then you ask your team for greater performance. If asked, people will generally feel that they are working hard now and that there is little or no room for improvement. It is stressed that team leaders must decide the level of performance they wish to achieve in their team. It is the same process as a coach working with an athlete. If the judgement is that the athlete is better than he or she is achieving, then the coach must place that athlete under the appropriate, balanced pressure. The coach sets the standard and draws acceptance from the athlete that if the right things are done at the right time, then the standard will be realised. This is a highly emotionally circumstance, triggered by the creative statement. The coach must be firm in the face of 'but we are working hard already'.

At that point, business is not a democracy. It is the great

leader/coach who draws people beyond their comfort zones and guides their achievement to levels they did not think were possible. They feel good, the coach feels good and the results are good. But these strong, satisfied feelings are after the event. The leader/coach must be firm, with insight, understanding and the strength of patience, and must show the way through the tensions and uncertainties that inevitably result when a team sets high targets for itself.

Bridging the gap between knowing how to do it and doing it

The process to use is one of people applying the skills and understanding they have. Seldom are people making the most of that which they already know and understand. Frequently I hear managers say 'but they have been trained'. Seek to bridge this gap between what people know and what they do. Focus can be one of improving performance, rather than on 'training them' – reshaping their behaviour on the job with the tools they have, rather than training them in the tools in the first place.

Training and development using own job as a case study

The process is a blend of facilitation and consulting. The team is undergoing training in the sense that general principles are reviewed and discussed. The vehicle for facilitating the discussion is a case study that happens to be their own team and the jobs of the people in the workshop. This process is very effective, bringing to the fore the practical, real-world issues of accountability, politics, focus and urgency so difficult to reproduce in a typical training environment.

Beginning with the Management Team

I repeatedly find that an effective place to start is with the Management Team and key staff. This is the key team of any business. Whether it consists of two people or twenty, the focus, urgency and drive of this team will profoundly effect the performance of the business. Some of the questions to be confronted include the following.

- Is it possible to target more operating profit?
- Are we stretching ourselves in the manner we expect of our people?
- As a leadership team of the business, can we be more effective?
- Can we be more creative?

The output is a plan showing how the operating profit is to be improved in the coming twelve months. The amount of the improvement is decided on by the team leader – this I call the *'creative statement'*. Typical would be 'increase operating profit next financial year by £250,000 over and above current budgets and over and above current expectations'. There are two rules: (1) there is to be no capital expenditure; (2) the result is to be achieved by a balanced approach to revenue, direct costs and margin, and overheads. Effectively, the process begins with the profit profile of the business and the creative statement then focuses the team on how the profit profile can be improved. I find that when a team are asked, and expected to stretch their creativity and experience, that the opportunities are uncovered and the learning is significant with a resulting permanent change in the climate or culture of the team.

Sales team	Begins each day with an empty piece of paper and has an excellent day when they fill the paper with orders.
Operations team	Begins each day with a full piece of paper and has an excellent day when they get everything done.
Retail store team	Begins each day with the paper half full and has an excellent day when all the store and administrative work is done and they have given excellent customer service and filled the empty half of the paper with orders.
Management team	Has to make sure that each of the above teams that it is leading has as many excellent days as possible – and to make doubly sure that no team fails to have an excellent day due to anything the management team could have or should have done.

typical goals that would be set for a team seeking to
ormance.

tatement

To increase operating profit by **£100,000** over and above
current expectations and current budget in the current
financial year and for that to build into **£250,000** increase in
operating profit in the coming financial year.

Goals

☑ To use the demand for improved operating profit to focus, stretch and consolidate team performance.

☑ To review and consolidate team roles and accountabilities.

☑ To review the business processes arising for those roles and to redevelop as deemed appropriate.

☑ To improve each individual person's actioning of his or her role in the team.

☑ Consolidate team actions in relation to the agreed plans and strategy.

Begin by challenging yourself, then draw others in your team to challenge themselves. It is not a passive process, and at times you will hesitate in the face of the turmoil due to uncertainty. At these moments, only faith in oneself and belief in the importance of investing in oneself will provide the needed strength. But if you quietly, gently, firmly just do it, you will be rewarded with greater leadership prowess, better business results and deeper satisfaction with yourself.

Where to Start?

The Need for Focus

It is crucial for key team members to have an accepted and shared conceptual formula that focuses attention on the crucial factors that determine operating profit. The team also needs to develop insight into the interrelationship of those factors and how to manage them to optimise and increase operating profit.

Make It Happen

The difference between administering a business and managing a business is that the administrator merely maintains the status quo. In the modern business environment, that is not enough: the business needs management committed to making things happen to ensure that the business maintains its customers, profits and return on capital.

Accountability

The aim of the management team is to generate sales revenue and turn it into operating profit. Within this, each team member has more particular accountabilities. Specifically, each team member must understand which lines and which parts of lines they are accountable for within the agreed profit profile of the business. It is then the responsibility of that manager to develop the insight, skills and control to manipulate those factors and so allow all members to fulfil their roles within the team's overall aim.

Where team members have a general supporting role – an old-fashioned staff function such as the accountant or HR manager – then the role is defined in those terms, for instance, providing historical data and data projecting the impact of management decisions.

Developing the Team Climate

Managers expect operations or a sales or customer service team to be focused on those factors that ensure that the team achieves its aim. Usually, the people are expected to participate, to stay on the topic, to not let personalities or politics get in the way of improving performance, to monitor performance closely – and to get on and do this with a minimum of supervision, with the team members providing peer pressure on performance. Often, however, the functioning of the management team itself does not follow these ethics.

Then where to start? Start with the management team going back to the basics of determining its aim (to turn revenue into operating profit) and the role of each team member within that aim; to establish a clear profit formula; and for all managers to focus vigorously on managing their portfolios and maximising their contribution to the team's aim. Once these ethics become habit and the success is enjoyed and felt through the business, ask all teams to follow this lead.

> The aim of the management team is to generate sales revenue and turn it into operating profit

Some Crucial Questions

- Do you know the few but essential factors that determine profit and performance?
- Can you pinpoint precisely which changes have the best and worst impact on operating profit?
- Are you absolutely clear on what you need to do to maintain and improve profits?
- Are you absolutely clear what your people must do to improve profits?
- Are your people absolutely clear on what they must do?

Plenty of Activity, but Getting it Right is not Easy (Ref 6)
The following comments are from a US survey of major companies

- Over 50% of senior executives surveyed reported five or more change initiatives in the past 18 months.

- Over 50% reported employee attitudes, buy-ins or resistance to change as the concerns most likely to keep them awake at night.

- 67% of executives reported the initiatives had showed up on the bottom line.

- The employees saw it differently – 75% said their skills had not improved, 49% perceived a drop in morale, and while they generally agreed that profitability had improved, they saw the success of the initiatives as 20% less than their executive counterparts.

- Despite the above, less than 25% of the executives planned initiatives involving employee participation, leadership development, team development or performance systems development. There seems to be two attitudes:

  - making the business profitable in spite of the people, or
  - making the business profitable through the people.

Evidence is accumulating that operating profit is stronger and more consistent when the people are actively supportive of the company and management. (Ref. 1, 2, 3, 4, 5, 6, 7, 8, 9, 10, 11, 12, 13, 14, 15, 16)

Controlling Operating Profit (Ref. 17, 18, 19, 20, 21)

What is Operating Profit?
It is the profit before deductions for interest and income tax, and before any extraordinary gains and losses. Operating profit is sometimes called EBIT: Earnings Before Interest and Tax. It is a direct measure of how well the management managed the resources under their control.

Turning sales revenue into operating profit is the priority aim of a management team.

Need for a Clear, Practical Focus
Too often management reports contain too much detail. A management team needs a simple formula that contains the critical factors effecting operating profit, and by monitoring this formula the management team can focus its efforts to ensure operating profit is maintained and increased.

A management team needs a simple formula whereby it orientates itself to its priority aim. Each person in the management team needs to have a clearly defined responsibility for one or several lines in the formula or even just a part of one line. The summary formula is then supported by detailed reports whereby managers review the performance of the teams and determine necessary action. The Profit Profile (Ref.17) provides the necessary formula.

The Profit Profile and Operating Profit (Ref 17)

Sales Price	100%
Product Cost	50%
Variable Expenses	12%
Gross Profit	38%
Fixed Expenses	28%
Operating Profit **10%**	

Operating profit is the small difference between two much larger numbers, sales revenue and expenses. Small changes in either have much larger impact on operating profit.

Exercise: In the diagram below, the current ratios are shown as percentages. The second column shows the changes effected by a 1% increase in sales and a 1% decrease in each of the three expenses. Complete a similar exercise with the ratios for your own business.

	Current ratios	*1 % change*
Sales	100	101
Product cost	50	49.5
Variable expenses	12	11.88
Gross margin	38	39.62
Fixed expenses	28	27.72
Operating profit	10	11.9

A 1% sales revenue increase combined with a 1% expenses decrease produces a 19% improvement in operating profit.

Not Just Historical Review

It is not enough for management teams to review historical performance via the formula. They also need a means of projecting the effects on operating profit of planned and unplanned changes in the factors effecting operating profits. The profit profile provides this proactive planning tool.

A Simple Example

Suppose we are running a fast foods van. We sell a range of products with the average sales revenue of £15.00 per litre. The product costs £4.00 per litre. There are variable expenses – spoons, napkins, straws and toppings – of £1.00 per litre. We have a sales volume of 5,000 litres. Our fixed expenses – petrol, depreciation, repairs and maintenance, mobile phone, insurance – are £30,000 per year (These figures ignore goods and services and other value added taxes)

Profit margin per unit – the key to operating profit		Calculating operating profit	
Sales revenue per litre	£15.00	Profit margin	£10.00
Product cost	£4.00	Sales volume	5,000 litres
Variable expenses	£1.00	Total profit margin	£50,000
Profit margin per litre	£10.00	Fixed expenses	£30,000
		Operating profit	£20,000
Profit margin/ unit is the essential starting point for building sustainable operating profit.		The essential steps are to multiply the sales margin by the sales volume.	

Calculate the break-even

The break-even is the volume of sales need to cover the fixed expenses. This can be obtained by dividing the fixed expenses by the profit margin per litre, that is: £30,000/£10 = 3,000 litres

Allocation of Fixed Costs or Overheads

A second method of calculating operating profit is to allocate fixed costs to each unit sold. In the example, £30,000 allocated over 5,000 litres is £6.00 per litre. We can then calculate operating profit by calculating the operating profit per litre, (£10.00 less £6.00 gives £4.00) multiplied by sales volume.

In this introduction we will not consider overhead allocation methods. The types of problems that occur are well illustrated by our van business. For example, a sundae takes more time, effort and so on than a single cone; should it be allocated more overhead or not? Throughout this book series, overhead will be treated as a burden on the business to be recovered by profit margin per unit multiplied by sales volume. break-even is defined as the point at which this formula equals overhead costs.

Simple Concepts Well Applied

Being able to understand, analyse and manipulate the basics of operating profit is important. Not being able to is like a marketing manager not understanding positioning or an accountant not knowing the difference between debt and equity.

The concept promoted here is to create insightful, simple concepts and apply them constantly, thoroughly.

Profit Sensitivity (Ref 17)

The profit profile contains a summary of the factors that have most impact on profit. It can now be used to assess the effect on operating profit to planned and unplanned changes. In the following examples the factors are varied one at a time. This seldom happens – normally a change in costs affects price which affects volume. Changes in several variables are analysed in the following sections. We will continue to use the van business example.

```
┌─────────────────────────────────────────────────────────────────────┐
│                   The  Profit  Profile                                │
│                                                                       │
```

The Profit Profile

		Per unit	Total
Annual break-even volume			3,000 litres
Annual sales volume			5,000 litres
Sales revenue		£15.00	£75,000
Less:	Product code	£4.00	£209,000
	Variable expenses	£1.00	£15,000
Equals:	Profit margin	£10.00	£50,000
Less:	Fixed expenses		£30,000
Equals:	Operating profit		**£20,000**

Notes:

1. Includes break-even and sales volumes not included in conventional incomes statements

2. Variable expenses are separated

3. Per unit values are included

4. It is quick and easy to update

5. It keeps attention focused on the critical factors that most impact on profits

6. It is a simple format that provides a focus for the whole management team.

7. It avoids too much detail and so guides the management team to make the best decisions on profit maintenance.

10% Sales Volume Increase

Only items that change are shown in the 'changes' column of the Profit Profile.

	Before		Changes
Annual break-even volume	3,000 litres		
Annual sales volume	5,000 litres		540 litres
	Per unit	Total	Total
Sales revenue	£15.00	£75,000	£7,500
Less: Product costs	£4.00	£20,000	£2,000
Variable expenses	£1.00	£5,000	£500
Equals: Profit margin	£10.00	£50,000	£5,000
Less: Fixed expenses		£30,000	
Equals: Operating profit		**£20,000**	**£5,000**

The main question raised here is whether the business has the production capacity to handle such an increase in volume. To deal with this question we can adjust the profit profile and add "capacity volume" which is defined as the volume able to be produced without altering fixed expenses.

10% Sales Price Increase

	Before		**Changes**	
Capacity volume		6,000		
Break-even volume		3,000	-391	
Sales volume		5,000		
	Per unit	Total	Per unit	Total
Sales revenue	£15.00	£75,000.00	£1.50	£7,500.00
Less: Product costs	£4.00	£20,000.00		
Variable expenses	£1.00	£5,000.00		
Equals: Profit margin	£10.00	£50,000.00	£1.50	£7,500.00
Less: Fixed expenses		£30,000.00		
Equals: Operating profit		**£20,000.00**		**£7,500.00**

With the price increase, there is a noticeably greater impact than the volume increase. That is because the sales price increase improves the profit margin per unit. As a result, the break-even is decreased. Managers know these relationships, but too often forget the magnitude of the swings in operating profit resulting from quite small changes in profit margin per unit.

In this example, the operating profit increased 37.5% from a 10% increase in profit margin. It follows that every 1% improvement in profit margin increases operating profit 3.75%.

> **How would your shareholders react to a 4% increase in profits over budget?**
>
> **Do you know the sensitivity of your business to the types of changes above?**
>
> **How sharply are you and the management team focused on the art of the possible?**
>
> **How committed are you to achieving best possible?**

Understanding the Multiplier Effect of Changes on Operating Profit

A 10% increase in volume produced a 25% increase in operating profit. Why? This is because the profit margin for the first 3,000 litres merely covered fixed expenses. Above break-even, the total profit margin per unit becomes operating profit. Thus the percentage increase in operating profit reflects the percentage increase above break-even, not the percentage increase in overall volume.

Managers instinctively understand these issues but frequently overlook the magnitude of potential changes to operating profit. Intensity and focus tend to diminish as sales stretch beyond break-even, where in fact intensity and focus should increase because every sale above break-even has a multiplier effect on profits.

This multiplier does not operate as dramatically in all businesses. This will be illustrated by analysing our van business. Managers need to understand the multiplier effects for their own business

10% Product Cost Increase

		Before		Changes	
Capacity volume		6,000			
Break-even volume		3,000	+125 litres		
Sales volume		5,000			
	Per unit	Total		Per unit	Total
Sales revenue	£15.00	£75,000.00			
Less: Product costs	£4.00	£20,000.00		(£0.4)	(£2,000)
Variable expenses	£1.00	£5,000.00			
Equals: Profit margin	£10.00	£50,000.00		(£0.4)	(£2,000)
Less: Fixed expenses		£30,000.00			
Equals: Operating profit		**£20,000.00**			**(£2,000)**

Profit falls 10% in line with an increase of 10% in costs.

Exercise:

1. Calculate the impact of a 10% product cost decrease.
2. Calculate the impact of a 10% increase in:
   (a) variable expenses (b) fixed expenses.

Summary

For a product based business:

1. A sales price change has a much greater effect than a sales volume change.

2. Both sales price and volume changes have a multiplier effect on operating profit.

3. Product cost, variable and fixed expense changes have the same percentage effect on operating profit.

Applying the Profit Profile to Different Businesses (Ref 17)

Every Business is the Same but Different

Managers and management teams typically believe their business to be different. They are right in the same sense that every person is different, but we all eat, breathe and have relationships.

The profit profile focuses on the basics and reflects how well the management has applied itself to the priority aim of converting sales revenue into operating profit.

Must Understand the Niche

Within any industry, there are certain success factors common to all businesses; but each business places different emphasis on each factor. For example, in food retailing the factors include price, service level and store style or presentation. A full service supermarket blends these elements one way while a discount warehouse market chooses another pattern.

The profit profile reflects the success of management in implementing these different operational philosophies.

Internal Creative Focus

The profit profile provides a tool to focus work teams on what they can do to influence the factors in the profit profile so that operating is improved.

Sales Revenue Variable Costs

Not all variable costs are related to volume. There are variable costs which are related to sales revenue. These include discounts, commissions and rebates. Variable expenses may need to be split in the profit profile.

Retailers and Wholesalers

The product cost is the cost of purchase of the goods. Variable costs could include ticketing, discounts and sales prices, and the cost of electronic security devices attached to products. Typically, retailers and wholesalers operate on a mark-up system, with product cost being a major factor in the profit profile.

Service Businesses
The main differences with a service business are as follows.

- Product cost is much lower than for other businesses.
- There are high fixed costs
- Variable costs can be on both volume and revenue – for example, sales discount and the cost of soap, towels and bathrobes in a hotel.
- Sales volume is expressed as a % of capacity – % of seats filled on an airline or rooms in a hotel

10% Volume Increase – Service Business Profit Profile

	Before	Changes
Sales volume % of capacity	80%	10%
Sales revenue	£500,000	£50,000
Variable expenses		
Sales	(£30,000)	(£3,000)
Sales volume	(£15,000)	(£1,500)
Product cost	(£20,000)	(£2,000)
Profit margin	£435,000	£43,500
Fixed expenses	360000	
Operating profit	£75,000	£43,500

Exercise:
1. Calculate the effect of a 10% price increase.

Calculating break-even for service business
The break-even for a service business is calculated in the same way as for a product-based business but based on each percentage point of

capacity. In the "Service Business Profit Profile" example above, we can calculate the profit margin on each percentage point of capacity.

Service Business Break-even

	Per % point
Sales revenue	£6,250
Variable expenses	
Sales £	(£300)
Sales volume	(£150)
Product cost	(£200)
Profit margin	£5,600

Therefore the break-even capacity is 64.3%. (It takes 64.3% of capacity to cover the fixed expenses of £360,000)

Profit Sensitivity of service business

For a service business with low product cost, a volume increase has almost as much effect as a price increase. This is in contrast to product based businesses where a price increase has a much greater impact on operating profit than a volume increase.

These differences become important in the following section on strategies and tactics.

Manufacturing Product Cost

The product cost for manufacturers must be calculated. It is the central focus of the factory or operations team in a manufacturing business.

Manufacturing Cost Profile

Practical capacity		12,000 units
Actual output		10,000 units
	Total	**Per unit**
Raw materials	£1,000,000	£100.00
Packaging	£150,000	£15.00
Direct labour	£1,500,000	£150.00
Variable overhead	£300,000	£30.00
Fixed overhead	£1,600,000	£160.00
Total manufacturing cost	£4,550,000	£455.00

Notes

1. The output potential capacity is the output potential without further investment or without increasing fixed overheads

2. Product cost per unit is a calculated amount and depends on accurate information on costs and output.

3. The cost per unit is an average cost involving only manufacturing costs

Idle Capacity Cost

In the previous example, fixed overhead is distributed over actual output giving £160 per unit. The idle capacity (2000 units) is acknowledged as a sales opportunity. It is accepted that the fixed costs may be spread over the practical product capacity. If so, the Manufacturing Cost Profile would need to show "Idle Capacity Cost" – this cost however is not necessarily controllable by the manufacturing team.

Multiple products

Total manufacturing costs can be aggregated across many products to give the averaged costs of the manufacturing unit. Alternatively the manufacturing cost profile can be applied to each product line. Where this is done, care must be taken in allocating fixed manufacturing costs. Any such allocation can only be arbitrary. What is preferred is to treat each product as providing a contribution to manufacturing fixed overhead.

To create a profit profile for each product line, the manufacturing overhead can be allocated; this is best done using some common denominator such as direct labour or materials. Based on such allocations, product lines can appear unprofitable and great care needs to be taken lest inappropriate decisions be made.

Product Line Profit Profile

	Economy	Standard	Deluxe	Average/ Totals
Sales price	£50.00	£60.00	£70.00	£58.33
Product cost	(£28.50)	(£35.50)	(£38.00)	(£33.58)
Variable expense	(£3.00)	(£5.00)	(£7.00)	(£4.67)
Profit margin/unit	£18.50	£19.50	£25.00	£20.08
Sales volume	20,000	30,000	10,000	50,000
Total profit margin	£370,000	£585,000	£250,000	£1,205,000
Fixed expenses		(£8,450,000)		
Operating profit		£360,000		

Notes:

1. It is often helpful to show percentages in this report.

2. Manufacturing fixed overheads is not allocated across products but is treated as part of fixed operating expenses.

Because product is capitalised as inventory, it is important to know accurately which costs are classified product costs.

Turnaround (Ref. 17)

Profit Profile for Turnaround

	Per unit	Total
Sales volume		60,000
Break-even volume		73,400
Capacity volume		80,000
	Per unit	**Total**
Sales revenue	£40.00	£2,400,000
Product cost	(£26.00)	(£1,560,000)
Variable cost	(£8.00)	(£480,000)
Profit margin	£6.00	£360,000
Fixed expenses		(£440,000)
Operating profit (loss)		(£80,000)

Analysis

1. Fixed expenses at 18% of revenue are high. If this was the division of a large business, and an element of fixed expense was allocated, this would need to be reviewed. Each element of fixed expenses needs to be reviewed.

2. Break-even is 91.75% of total capacity. This is also very high.

3. Even at 100% of capacity the operating profit will only be £40,000 (£6 x 80,000 units – fixed expenses) or 1.7% of sales. This is very low.

Actions

It is possible to correct the situation by loading all the necessary improvements onto one factor such as sales price or a reduction in advertising. This type of corrective action usually distorts the business and may jeopardise the business in the long term. The price increase necessary to generate an operating profit of £100,000 assuming no change in volume is £43 or a 7.5% price increase. This is large and could certainly effect volume.

A balanced approach to the turnaround is preferable. Below is the profit profile for a 1% improvement in all of the key factors.

One Percent Improvement in each Profit Margin Factor

Sales volume				60,000
Break-even volume				73,400
Capacity volume				80,000

	Before per unit	Per unit	Total	Changes
Sales revenue	£40.00	£40.40	£2,424,000	£24,000
Product cost	(£26.00)	(£25.74)	(£154,400)	£15,600
Variable cost	(£8.00)	(£7.92)	(£475,200)	(£4,800)
Fixed expenses			(£435,600)	£4,400
Operating profit (loss)			(£31,200)	£48,800

Each 1% improvement increases operating profit by £48,800. Therefore a 4% improvement in each of the factors will improve operating profit by £195,200 and turn the loss (£80,000) into a profit of £115,200. The key aim of the management team in this turnaround must be to improve the profit margin per unit to at least £8, preferable £10.

Exercise: Calculate the percentage changes you would need to make to produce an operating profit of £150,000.

Controlling Profit Erosion (Ref. 17)

Sales Factors

Rebates, discounts, coupons
• Are discounts built into your computer pricing?
• When were they last reviewed?
• Does your sales team give discounts in units of 5%, 10%?
• Can they be guided to offer 2%, 4%?
• Can each of your salespeople identify ten clients where discounts could be reduced without loss of volume?

- Can your sales team be guided to sell the benefits and retain margin?

Product Cost

Waste, rework, repairs, shrinkage
- Are losses and waste accurately recorded?
- Are the main problem areas identified?
- What actions would reduce waste and rework by 25%?
- How can warranties and returns be reduced 50%?
- How can recalls be eliminated?

Administration

Lost discounts, misinformation
- What costs are incurred due to wrong or incomplete information?
- Do you ever lose out on volume or prompt payment discounts?
- Do debtors ever hold up payments because of errors in invoices or packing advices?

Strategies and Tactics

Using the Profit Profile to Assess the Impact of Changes on Operating Profit
The commercial environment is not static. Competitive pressures increase, raw materials increase in price, some competitors become vulnerable.

- Should we drop prices to gain market share ?
- Should we increase price? How much volume could we stand to use?
- Should the product cost increase be passed on? How can we assess potential effects?

> ### *The Profit Profile can be used to Explore "What if...." questions.*
>
> Care is required in estimating the volume change as a consequence of any price change.
>
> Actions supporting this judgement could include :
>
> • team brainstorming with all managers, or sales staff
>
> • questionnaires to customers
>
> • formal market research

Three issues will now be examined.

Tactic 1.   Decrease in sales price to gain volume
Tactic 2.   Increase in sales price with a loss of volume
Tactic 3.   Passing on a materials cost increase with a loss of volume

Tactic 1: Decrease price, gain volume

This is a bad idea for product-based businesses. Typically the increase in volume has to be very large to offset even a modest price drop. The reason is that the small drop in sales price becomes a large decrease in profit margin per unit.

> The management team in a product based business needs to protect profit margin per unit and NOT give it away.

Service businesses suffer much less. There is a small drop in profits, so the risk of gaining the extra volume to increase profits is possibly justified. Even so, the move needs to be supported by a careful analysis of where the new business will come from – customer by customer – and preferably tried first with several customers.

10% Sales Price Decrease with 10% Sales Volume Increase

Product Business

	Before		After	
Break-even volume	36,700		55,000	
Sales volume	60,000		66,000	

	Per unit	Total	Per unit	Total
Sales revenue	£40.00	£2,400,000	£36.00	£2,376,000
Product cost	(£22.00)	(£1,320,000)	(£22.00)	(£1,452,000)
Variable expenses	(£6.00)	(£360,000)	(£6.00)	(£396,000)
Profit margin	£12.00	£720,000	£8.00	£528,000
Fixed expenses		(£440,000)		(£440,000)
Operating profit		£280,000		£88,000

Exercise: Calculate the volume increase needed to offset the 10% price decrease

Answer: At the new profit margin per unit of £8, the volume would need to be 90,000 units to generate the £720,000 of total profit margin.

Service Business

	Before	After
Volume as % of capacity	80%	88%
Sales revenue	£2,080,000	£2,059,200
Product cost	(£80,000)	(£88,000)
Variable expenses	(£120,000)	(£132,000)
Profit margin	£1,880,000	£1,839,200
Fixed expenses	(£1,600,000)	(£1,600,000)
Operating profit	£280,000	£239,200

Note: Each percentage point was worth £26,000, but is now worth £23,400, thus reducing revenue (at 88%) to £2,059,200

Tactic 2: Increase price, lose volume

This is a good idea for product businesses. The increased profit comes from the large increase in profit margin per unit. But how many companies will give up volume to become more profitable? Most sales managers wouldn't hear of it. There are a host of side benefits –

for example the company gets more focused on core clients; service improves; quality improves; and morale improves. Growth can then again proceed based on strong word of mouth.

This tactic is not effective in service businesses unless the drop in volume enables a reduction in fixed expenses.

10% Sales Price Increase with 10% Sales Volume Decrease

Product Business

	Before		After	
Break-even volume	36,700		27,500	
Sales volume	60,000		54,000	

	Per unit	Total	Per unit	Total
Sales revenue	£40.00	£2,400,000	£44.00	£2,376,000
Product cost	(£22.00)	(£1,320,000)	(£22.00)	(£1,188,000)
Variable expenses	(£6.00)	(£360,000)	(£6.00)	(£324,000)
Profit margin	£12.00	£720,000	£16.00	£864,000
Fixed expenses		(£440,000)		(£440,000)
Operating profit		£280,000		£424,000

Exercise: Calculate the decrease needed to offset the 10% increase in price

Answer: At the new profit margin per unit of £16, the volume would need fall to 45,000 units to generate the £720,000 of total profit margin.

Service Business

	Before	After
Volume as % of capacity	80%	88%
Sales revenue	£2,080,000	£2,059,200
Product cost	(£80,000)	(£72,000)
Variable expenses	(£120,000)	(£108,000)
Profit margin	£1,880,000	£1,879,200
Fixed expenses	(£1,600,000)	(£1,600,000)
Operating profit	£280,000	£279,200

Note: New percentage volume value £286,000 per point

Service businesses: The action is in revenue and fixed expenses. If revenue can be increased without losing volume or increasing fixed expenses, then profits will improve dramatically.

Tactic 3 Product Cost Increase – Pass On or Not?

A 10% Product Cost Increase Passed On to Customers with an 8% Decrease in Volume

Product Business

	Before		After	
Break-even volume	36,700		36,700	
Sales volume	60,000		55,200	

	Per unit	Total	Per unit	Total
Sales revenue	£40.00	£2,400,000	£42.20	£2,329,440
Product cost	(£22.00)	(£1,320,000)	(£24.20)	(£1,335,840)
Variable expenses	(£6.00)	(£360,000)	(£6.00)	(£331,200)
Profit margin	£12.00	£720,000	£12.00	£662,400
Fixed expenses		(£440,000)		(£440,000)
Operating profit		£280,000		£222,400

Note: This analysis is the same as for a price increase with volume reduction

Establish the profit profile of your business
(1)

	Per unit	Total
Capacity volume (2)		
Sales volume (3)		
Sales volume as % of capacity (3)		
Break-even volume (4)		
Sales revenue		
Product cost		
Raw materials (5)		
Consumables		
Direct labour		
Manufacturing variable cost		
Total product cost		
Variable operating expenses		
Profit margin		
Fixed expenses		
Operating (6)		
Manufacturing		
Operating profit		

Notes:
1. Use only those lines appropriate for your business.
2. This is the volume available without plant changes or increase in fixed costs.

3. Use one or the other depending on whether product or service type business.
4. This can be expressed as % of capacity for service businesses.
5. This can be in a separate, supporting reports.
6. Manufacturing cost profile report.
7. This can be in separate, supporting reports.

Questions:

1. What % volume is break-even?
2. Is it low enough?
3. Is the profit to sales ratio high enough?
4. What is a good industry standard?
5. What factors are eroding profits?
   - discounts and rebates
   - waste
   - rework and poor quality
   - misinformation
   - other ...

Assessing Sensitivity and Key Trade Offs

If necessary, do a Profit Profile to establish profit margins for each product group. Then add total profit margin for each product group to get company total profit margin

1. Calculate decreasing product cost 5%, increasing prices 1% and decreasing fixed cost 5%.

	Before		After	
Capacity volume (2)				
Sales volume (3)				
Sales volume as % of capacity (3)				
Break-even volume (4)				
	Per unit	Total	Per unit	Total
Sales revenue				
Product cost				
Raw materials (5)				
Consumables				
Direct labour				
Manufacturing variable cost				
Total product cost				
Variable operating expenses				
Profit margin				
Fixed expenses				
Operating (6)				
Manufacturing				
Operating profit				

2. Calculate decreasing prices 5% while increasing volume 5%

	Before		After	
Capacity volume (2)				
Sales volume (3)				
Sales volume as % of capacity (3)				
Break-even volume (4)				
	Per unit	Total	Per unit	Total
Sales revenue				
Product cost				
Raw materials (5)				
Consumables				
Direct labour				
Manufacturing variable cost				
Total product cost				
Variable operating expenses				
Profit margin				
Fixed expenses				
Operating (6)				
Manufacturing				
Operating profit				

3. Calculate increasing prices 5% while decreasing volume 5%

	Before		After	
Capacity volume (2)				
Sales volume (3)				
Sales volume as % of capacity (3)				
Break-even volume (4)				
	Per unit	Total	Per unit	Total
Sales revenue				
Product cost				
Raw materials (5)				
Consumables				
Direct labour				
Manufacturing variable cost				
Total product cost				
Variable operating expenses				
Profit margin				
Fixed expenses				
Operating (6)				
Manufacturing				
Operating profit				

4. Calculate the practical changes that will increase operating profit 25%.

Don't load too much on any single factor; keep the business in balance. Use your judgement to assess changes you believe are practical. The increase of 25% to be over and above your 'best estimate' of the profit for the current year. The increase to be achieved without capital expenditure.

	Before		After	
Capacity volume (2)				
Sales volume (3)				
Sales volume as % of capacity (3)				
Break-even volume (4)				
	Per unit	Total	Per unit	Total
Sales revenue				
Product cost				
Raw materials (5)				
Consumables				
Direct labour				
Manufacturing variable cost				
Total product cost				
Variable operating expenses				
Profit margin				
Fixed expenses				
Operating (6)				
Manufacturing				
Operating profit				

Identifying Likely Projects

From your notes and analyses identify the six projects that would achieve an increase in operating profit of at least 25%. Identify those projects under your direct control.

Project	Action/comment
1	
2	
3	
4	
5	
6	

The Business Growth Spread Sheet

A budget is the core of any business planning. It should portray a conservative, realistic expectation of what will happen. It needs to be quite detailed, representing the thinking out of the details of the business operations and the financial consequences of those operations.

The details in a budget are at once its strength and its weakness. Too often I find management teams bogged in the detail, and not retaining enough of an overview, too lost in working in the business and with not enough focus of working on the business. For this reason I have developed the business growth spread sheet. The spreadsheet is in three sections as shown below.

The budget or best estimate of the result for the current financial year	The summary of the projects to be implemented and the effect on the profit profile factors this financial year and the next financial year.	The target for this financial year as a result of the projects and the flow-on effect of the projects into the next financial year.

The concept assumes achievement of the budget as the base. The projects are then those activities selected by the management team whereby the team aims to add momentum to the business this year with a flow on effect into next year.

Business Growth Plan for

				Years					
Budget or best estimate		Projects and their effects						Projected after-effect of projects	
			Current year effects		Year 1 effects			Current year £	Year 1 £
Profit profile	Opening	Sales Projects	Sales	Costs	Sales	Costs			
	£		£	£	£	£			
Revenue		1	£	£	£	£			
		2	£	£	£	£			
		3	£	£	£	£			
		4	£	£	£	£			
		Total sales change	£		£				
		Direct costs change from sales projects		£		£			
		Direct cost projects							
Direct costs		1		£		£			
		2		£		£			
		3		£		£			
		4		£		£			
		Total direct cost changes		£		£			
Gross profit									
		Overhead projects							
Overheads		1		£		£			
		2		£		£			
		3		£		£			
		4		£		£			
		Total overhead changes		£		£			
Operating profit									
% gross profit	%							%	%
% profit to sales	%							%	%
£ increase in profit									

There are two crucial questions about the budget that forms the basis for this spreadsheet. (1) How is the budget set? (2) What happens if the team gets into the year and finds it is behind budget?

The budget is set with the central idea in mind that a business is like a fly wheel – it has a certain existing inertia not that difficult to keep going. So the budget for next financial year could begin with this year's result then be increased or decreased based on projected economic activity and projected competitor activity. So, for example, the budget might be a 3% growth in revenues over last year, no significant increase in overheads, and with the same margin giving a 6% increase in operating profit. This is of course quite modest, but reflects the momentum of the business. Now, the management team reviews the projects, selects those offering the best pay-back this year and with strong flow on into next year. This then increases revenue growth to 12%, with a improvement in margin and a reduction in overheads through better use of technology resulting in better business processes giving a 32% increase in operating profit.

Ensuring budget achievement

When a management team finds that the base budget is not being achieved, then it needs to quickly identify additional projects designed to recover the budget. The budget is the base, the projects then add momentum to the business to improve upon this base. It is important that the projects designed and agreed to add momentum are not then used to fill the hole in the budget, because then the management team has added no momentum to the business. A management team adopting this philosophy will very likely be in a state of 'nervous self-belief'. This as it should be for any team or individual committing him or herself to superior performance.

It is common for a management team adopting this philosophy to find ways for the business to achieve more revenue without significant increase in overhead and in part, this results from the management team itself being more effective at doing that which it needs to do. In simple terms, the cost of the management team remains constant while the revenue and profits increase. Almost invariably the emotional state of such teams is one of energy and excitement.

Challenges are faced and beaten – there is much nervous energy, pressure and stress. It is great when the result is achieved. For the directors overseeing such teams, it is crucial that they understand the strain of achievement and the potential for burnout from prolonged exposure to the energy of challenge and insist that all team members take an annual vacation of at least two weeks enabling complete revitalisation.

A strategy template

The business growth spreadsheet enables focus on those activities most adding to the bottom line. Typically, the base of the business is managed in a regular, steady manner while the projects receive 'extra focus and attention'. The spreadsheet was never intended as a strategy development document. However, by assessing the flow on of projects, the process enables projection of the business over two years and frequently I find that this is sufficient forward projection and no further strategic thinking need be done.

Each year, the budget is set based on last year and adjusted based on the estimate of economic and competitor activity, then the projects selected to add momentum and to improve operating profit, so that each year the management team does a two year strategic review. This is made more effective by ensuring a 'zero base' for all projects, that is any projects begun last year and not yet completed are then put in priority with all possible projects and may or may not become a priority for the coming year.

When using the spreadsheet this way, capital expenditure projects can be added, as can long term projects. For example, the decision to invest now in e-commerce knowing that this will increase overheads without commensurate increase in revenues or profits for two or maybe three or more years. For the purpose of annual accounts, long-term project expenditure would most likely be written off in the year incurred. For the purposes of the management team, long-term project expenditure should perhaps be shown as profits reinvested in an accumulating fund, and that eventually the team is expected to recover this fund and to show returns on the capital in the fund.

Business processes

When reviewing expense-based projects it is important to have a clear, simple model of the business in mind. What should be avoided are projects involving review of the list of expenses and cutting £100 there and £2,000 here and ...

The focus should be on the business processes. Imagine the business processes as a series of pipes and all the materials, product, information and movement of people is through these pipes. The expenses are a consequence of this movement and of the nature and shape of the pipes, so alter the pipes and the expenses will change. For example, imagine a customer services unit of ten people, responding to customers, taking orders and so on. An expense review might uncover some several thousand pounds in lost time and inefficient use of mobile phones, etc. Realising these savings will inevitably be difficult, generating resentment for 'pettiness' among the team. Detailed investigation of customer inquiries however might show that 40% involve queries about product – static information that customers themselves could research if the product information was on the internet – and that 60% of the team's time is devoted to such inquiries. An investment of say £100,000 to improve the product information on the world wide web could then result in a permanent reduction of two or even three in the team with an increase in focus and service. These results ignore any inefficiencies or misuse of mobile phones, all of which could easily be seen as 'perks' by team members.

A good starting point for identifying opportunities for improving business processes is to identify the hassles encountered by team members in their job, especially those that recur, then identifying the hassles encountered by customers. Most likely underlying a recurring hassle is a business process that could usefully be fixed so that the hassle does not occur, and simultaneously taking advantage to improve the outputs associated with the business process.

Identifying good profit to sales ratios

Recently, when prospecting for new clients I have been privileged to encounter two extremely well run businesses. I relate these anecdotes because of their effect on me. In short, these companies altered my view of what is a 'good result' and what is a 'great result'. Unfortunately I am not able to name the companies concerned, so you will have to accept my word that they exist.

The first company is in the newspaper industry, producing and distributing a number of local newspapers. Revenues are some £30 million, with investments in plant of some £20 million. The profit to sales ratio is 31%. When initially told this number I was incredulous, but was shown information that confirmed it. The second business is in the foundry industry. It has revenues of £3 million, with profit to sales of 30%. These are excellent results by any standard. How did they do it?

Both managing directors were quite willing to discuss how they achieved these results. The remarkable thing is that there is no great secret and certainly you will know all that is needed to do the same in your business. Both managing directors had a clear focus on business processes and the need to keep refining and improving those processes. In neither instance, were there high levels of technology involved. The focus was on correctly confronting every hassle when it occurred, and on involving the staff in finding and implementing the best possible solution. Both managers said that their staff in any section could tell me of the key business processes in that section, as well as the hassles and what was being done about them. With those profit to sales ratios I believed them. The foundry business could show me the book where every problem or hassle for the last ten years was recorded, with notes on what was done and who did it. Neither managing director was 'charismatic', but both shared a simple, focused discipline of daily identifying things to improve the operation of their business and clearly exhibited the day by day patience and discipline to do the few simple things they saw would add up to a better bottom line. The smoother the business process and the more the people understand and can implement them the fewer people you need and the more they can do.

You can do the same in your business. But it is not a 'quick fix'. The starting point is for you and your team members to begin and to quietly, patiently and progressively improve your profit to sales by implementing the tactics and philosophy outlined in these books.

Case study examples

Below are examples illustrating application of the ideas. All of the businesses showed improvements in operating profit and in the profit to sales ratio over periods ranging from four or five months to eighteen months. In all cases, the delay in results showing in the profit and loss figures was due to the rate at which the management team mastered the art of maintaining sufficient effective focus on the core of the business (to ensure budget) while generating extra focus and effort on the two or three projects to add momentum. The second important point is that the improvement in results did not always emerge from the projects nominated – that is, the team began with what it thought were the priority projects only to find that improved results popped out somewhere else, usually related to the beginning project. A consistent issue was keeping down the number of projects being worked on at any time. One is okay, three is hard and four is impossible. But it does depend on the nature of the project.

The final key point is for the top team to conceptualise what to implement within a project – that is, to identify the precise steps and who has to do them. Consistently I find that this exercise is left too general, and people are asked not only to act in a way most likely to achieve the result, but also to create their own concepts of what those actions should be. This vagueness is usually too much to ask and the result will be disappointing.

The principle guiding the identification of the actions most likely to achieve the result is that for every goal there are behaviours that must be acted out. It is the task of the management team to think out the actions that are most likely to achieve the result – this is a crucial part of the planning process. By getting behaviours clear, then the leadership team can guide people to do the things most likely to facilitate success, and to ensure an effective balance of the actions that maintain momentum (achieving budget) and then add to that momentum (focused, selective growth or profit development). This is well illustrated in the first case study. (See *The Five Steps to Effective Business Leadership* for a more detailed discussion on this issue.)

Case 1: Improving profitability in industrial products sales and distribution

This company had been a client for eight or ten years. For each of the last four years, we had implemented the philosophy above with management team workshops, usually of two days, in which the agreed forecast for the coming financial year was reviewed and projects identified to add profits. The first year had been a learning year for the team, and the results, while apparent, had not been spectacular. The second year was to have been expansive, but then came the Asian crisis, which was not predicted, and the comment made by the managing director was 'the projects saved the result'. The third year was very sound, but the focus had been on cost reduction because the economic climate was tight and had been predicted to be so. The year illustrated here is predicted to be quite expansive, in fact this is forecast for the coming two or three years. Therefore the team is now focused on growth and market share. The spreadsheet is below, the workshop was conducted two months before the commencement of the new financial year but after the budget had been agreed by the directors.

Business Growth Plan for ..... Industrial products distributor							Years 2000/2001	
Budget or best estimate		**Projects and their effects**					**Projected after-effect of projects**	
			Current year effects		**Year 1 effects**			
Profit profile	Opening	£ Sales Projects	Sales	Costs	Sales	Costs	Current year £	Year 1 £
Revenue	£9,700,000	1 Process equipment, new product line	£200,000	£100,000	£350,000	£190,000	£10,410,000	£11,610,000
		2 OEM producers	£150,000	£75,000	£250,000	£130,000		
		3 Key accounts and target clients	£260,000	£130,000	£350,000	£160,000		
		4 Improving service, improving stock accuracy	£100,000	£50,000	£250,000	£130,000		
		Total sales change			£1,200,000			
		Direct costs change from sales projects		£335,000		£635,000		
		Direct cost projects						
Direct costs	£4,753,000	1		£		£	£5,108,000	£5,743,000
		2		£		£		
		3		£		£		
		4		£		£		
		Total direct cost changes		£335,000		£635,000		
Gross profit	£4,947,000						£5,302,000	£5,867,000
		Overhead projects						
Overheads	£3,735,000	1 Allow for overhead ascalation		£115,000		£115,000	£3,735,000	£3,850,000
		2		£		£		
		3		£		£		
		4		£		£		
		Total overhead changes		£115,000		£115,000		
Operating profit	£1,212,000						£1,567,000	£2,017,000
% gross profit	% 51.00						% 50.93	% 50.53
% profit to sales	% 12.49						% 15.05	% 17.37
£ increase in profit							**£355,000**	**£805,000**

Below are the notes that were circulated with the spreadsheet after the meeting. There are two crucial points to note: (1) the clear and firm separation between regional managers focused on sales and the MD and rest of the management team focused on improving service; (2) the way in which the sales team is focused to ensure the best possible chance of achieving the focused growth.

Notes as agreed

1. Spread sheet attached. The strategic philosophy embodied is to secure market share over the next two or three years, while allowing some gradual easing of margins. Margin pressure to come from (1) product increasingly a commodity. (2) Internationally available pricing from the internet.

2. If the team focuses on and achieves the results as presented in the spreadsheet over the coming two years, this would be a significant consolidation of the business in its market.

3. Major effort to be placed on improving customer service as this will become the key point of differentiation. This thrust to be lead by MD. For example, deal finally with stock accuracy.

4. Regional managers to focus and be facilitated to focus on market share and sales team effectiveness.

5. Key coaching issues for regional managers summarised as follows.

✓ Sales people must be guided to see where growth can come from.

✓ Must not present growth in terms of simple percentage.

✓ Must focus on the behaviours most likely to achieve result.

✓ Example; consider a sales territory as below.

✓ This type of analysis needs to be done for every territory, then all salespeople will 'see' clearly how to achieve the best possible result in their territory.

✓ The sales growth for the business can then arise by adding the results for each territory. BUT I REPEAT IT NEEDS TO BE DONE AS OUTLINED BELOW. OTHERWISE THIS SORT OF TARGETED GROWTH WILL NOT OCCUR.

Territory No 1	Revenue	Comment on behaviour needed
Sales last year 1999	£270,000	Taken as the base
Allow 2.5% growth	£6,750	Needs regular calling, good service and delivery, conscientious pursuing of opportunities
Process equipment sales 1999 were £2000. Target 2000 is £20,000.	£20,000	Need to identify likely customers where we can make extra sales without making an additional call on someone else. Regular and focused calling. Find out what they use and then pursue some or all of the business. Target to secure the sales from eight accounts.
OEM, key accounts and target clients –selecting and focusing on a few most likely to offer good sales increase. Last year a 30% increase from those accounts was targeted. This year, target eight accounts with last-year revenues of £80,000. Seek an increase this year of £15,000 or an 18.75% increase, which is less than the gains achieved last year.	£15,000	Need focused and effective calling, setting goals and targets for each of the eight selected accounts.
Total sales target 2000	£311,750	This is a 15.5% increase over last year. As such, it looks hard but each of the specific and targeted behaviours is realistic and the result achievable.

Summary of behaviours needed are:

      a. Regular calling on all clients with focus and purpose to ensure service and to secure additional business.

      b. Intensive, focused calling on process valve prospects. Likely no more than eight targets.

      c. Intensive focused calling on OEM or target clients or key accounts. Likely no more than eight targets.

6. The tone within the Management Team should be one of 'nervous self belief'. It is then crucial that this process is followed with the sales teams and they to end up in a state of nervous self belief. Then whenever one succeeds, the Regional Manager, Sales Director, and Managing Director all contribute as appropriate to the celebration of that success.

Case 2: Management Team consolidation

The second example was not specifically a profit improvement program. The aim was to consolidate and train a young and inexperienced management team. The business was in heavy engineering, manufacturing steel-formed products. Over a period of two years, there had been substantial reduction in staff numbers, major change in strategic focus and change in ownership. The new management team was now in place and the aim was to develop more effective teamwork and strengthen individual manager skills in relation to the role they held in the team.

Developing a manager does not occur without developing the person. Management skills are not something we slip on as we walk on the job each morning. There is some element of professional conduct, but there is also a strong element of personal development. Imagine coping with the death of someone very close. Some days we do not want to get out of bed, but we must. After coming through the grieving period, it is common for people to say how they feel they have grown – they feel stronger and able to cope with more than before. I believe that this is a result of the struggle to cope with the challenge of a situation where some days one is not sure of getting through the day. Growth of coping skills and self-assurance is brought about by the struggle of winning over a challenge. It is this that I believe leads to the other idea that success in sport makes for better and stronger men and women. I apply the philosophy in manager development by first establishing a challenging goal for the team that will stretch their skills and application. This can of course only be done in conjunction with the managing director, who must understand the process and accept it, and be quietly firm and committed in the face of the inevitable cries that they are working hard already. Once the creative challenge is established, the team is then offered coaching support and guidance in how to meet the challenge. For the great majority, it is an invigorating experience, but there are the occasional few for whom it is not.

The process begins with the business growth spreadsheet. This is a battle for such a team. The stretch required, the pressure of making something happen that otherwise will not, and the implicit questioning of their skills all result in creating an emotional and fractured environment. The process follows a quite predictable path from resistance, to grudging acceptance that more is possible, to passive resistance and an unaware failure to act, to a slow understanding of what it really takes to add momentum to a business. As these attitudes and emotions are settled, the team is also addressing its collective and individual skills and the need for an integrated effort if the result is really to be achieved. Teamwork is those actions by each person that will ensure the best possible result for the team – for a management team, that is the best possible operating profit. For each team member achieving the best possible result means doing all they can do to enhance operating profit and doing nothing that will undermine or detract from the efforts of any other team member. This in itself takes some time and discussion before it is understood and acted upon.

Slowly, steadily the team emerges into a state of nervous or anxious self-belief. A combination of understanding, seeing how it can be done and belief there are the skills in the team to do it. The spreadsheet that emerged is below.

Business Growth Plan for ..... Engineering business					Years 2000/2001			
Budget or best estimate		**Projects and their effects**	**Current year effects**		**Year 1 effects**		**Projected after-effect of projects**	
Profit profile	Opening £	Projects	Sales	Costs	Sales	Costs	Current year £	Year 1 £
Revenue	£10,308,000	**Sales Projects**					£10,683,000	£11,208,000
		1 Achieve better prices	£150,000		£250,000			
		2 Improve prospecting and coverage	£450,000	£375,000	£650,000	£546,000		
		3						
		4						
		Total sales change			£1,200,000			
		Direct costs change from sales projects		£375,000		£546,000		
Direct costs	£8,168,000	**Direct cost projects**					£8,248,000	£8,389,000
		1 Reduce steel waste	-£45,000		-£25,000			
		2 Improve productivity by better planning	-£150,000		-£100,000			
		3 Improve business processes in plant	-£100,000		-£200,000			
		4	3		3			
		Total direct cost changes	£335,000		£221,000			
Gross profit	£2,140,000						£2,435,000	£2,389,000
Overheads	£1,599,000	**Overhead projects**					£1,584,000	£1,544,000
		1 Reduce freight loss	-£15,000		-£35,000			
		2 Allow for overhead escalation			£75,000			
		3	£	3	£	3		
		4	£	3	£			
		Total overhead changes	-£15,000		-£40,000			
Operating profit	£541,000						£851,000	£1,275,000
% gross profit	%						%	%
% profit to sales	5%						8%	11.40%
£ increase in profit							£310,000	£234,000

63

Case 3: Improving retail profits

The final example is a straightforward project involving improving the profits in a small retail chain. The chain sold hardware, with four stores. It was run by a husband and wife team, the husband the managing director and operations director, the wife the administration and customer services manager. The chief point of interest is in the necessary expansion of the management team of the business and who should be included. Before the project, the 'management' was seen as the two owners, plus another person who looked after their small warehouse and was generally the purchasing manager. An important key to success in a retail chain is the skill and focus of the team leaders in each store. In the initial defining of this project, we agreed that the present management team became effectively the Board of Directors, and the new management team was to include the store team leaders. These people were not strictly managers, but they could and did have considerable influence on the focus and energy exhibited by the people in each of the stores.

The second crucial note in the spreadsheet is gaining understanding of the roles of each of the teams. It was agreed that the store teams would be accountable for the day-to-day feel, layout and energy in the store. These factors came to account in the percentage of people who came into the store and purchased something and came to account in the average invoice. Of the two, it was agreed that the average invoice was the most important. This was then to be increased by (1) reducing the level of discount offered to the trade customers who came into the stores and (2) by deliberately focusing on 'add on sales' with every sale. The head office or 'central team' as we agreed to call it, was responsible for the level of foot-traffic in the stores and for the overall range of product and product availability in the store. In short, the central team was expected to stock the store and provide foot-traffic and the store teams then had to ensure the store was presented so as to provide the best possible customer service and sales.

Business Growth Plan for ..... Retail hardware chain   **Years 2000/2001**

Profit profile	Budget or best estimate	Projects and their effects	Current year effects		Year 1 effects		Projected after-effect of projects	
	Opening	£ Sales Projects	Sales	Costs	Sales	Costs	Current year £	Year 1 £
Revenue	£8,400,000	1 Reduce discounting	£100,000		£150,000			
		2 Improve in-store selling	£150,000	£90,000	£250,000	£150,000		
		3 Introduce new range of product	£150,000	£90,000	£400,000	£240,000	£8,800,000	£9,600,000
		4						
		Total sales change	£400,000		£800,000			
		Direct costs change from sales projects		£180,000		£390,000		
		Direct cost projects						
Direct costs	£5,796,000	1 Improve buying on five key lines		-£35,000		-£40,000		
		2 Redce shrinkage from 2% to 1.4 and then 1%		-£50,000		-£34,000	£5,891,000	£6,207,000
		3		£		£		
		4		£		£		
		Total direct cost changes		£95,000		£316,000		
Gross profit	£2,604,000						£2,909,000	£3,393,000
		Overhead projects						
Overheads	£1,824,000	1 Improve goods handling, reduce staff by 2		-£60,000		£50,000		
		2 Cost of new range		£100,000		£90,000	£3,735,000	£3,850,000
		3 Overhead escalation		£		£		
		4		£		£		
		Total overhead changes		£115,000		£140,000		
Operating profit	£780,000						£1,045,000	£1,389,000
% gross profit	31%						33%	35.30%
% profit to sales	9.30%						11.90%	14.50%
£ increase in profit							**£265,000**	**£609,000**

Conclusion on case studies

In each case the business growth spreadsheet was supported first by a simple, one or two page strategic outline. This focused on what the business did, who the customers were, and what service the business would provide for those customers. The second document was an annual budget giving the detail of the costs and revenues. The business growth spreadsheet then enabled the key management team to firstly focus on achieving the budget and then on the extra creative and emotional effort to add momentum to the business.

Review of these examples will show the nature of the projects under different circumstances and how the spreadsheet summarises the detail and provides a simple yet effective reporting framework for the team.

References

1. Willmot, Peter, Total Quality with Teeth, TQM Magazine, Vol: 6, Issue: 4, 1994, pages 48-50

2. Bryan, Eugene L., Ongoing Change Management. Executive Excellence, Vol: 11, Issue: 4, April 1994, pages: 11-12

3. Rutledge, John, Just Do It, Forbes, Vol: 15, Issue: 4 , February 14 1994, page 142

4. Yandrick, Rudy M., Organizational Addiction, HR Magazine, Vol: 39 Issue: 12, December 1994, pages 92-95

5. Kanellos, Michael, Active management, Key to Success for Retailers. Computer Resellers News. Issue : 599, October 10 1994, pages 133-136

6. Kepner-Tregoe Consultancy, Surveys Reveal some Executives Ignore the Human Side of their Organizations. Canadian Manager. Vol: 19, Issue: 4 December 1994, page 20

7. Neisley, Joe, Learning the Ultimate Lesson in Partnering, Computer News, February 29 1994, page 108

8. Harrell, Wilson I, Slaying Giants, Success. Vol: 41, Issue: 8, October 1994, page 106

9. Harrison, D. Brian & Conn, Henry P., Mobilising Abilities through Teamwork, Canadian Business Review. Vol: 21, Issue: 3, Autumn 1994, pages 20-22

10. Mullin, Rick, Dictates for the Top, Suggestion from the Floor. Chemical Week, Vol: 155, Issue: 10, September 21, 1994, pages 33-36

11. Anonymous. Team Yakka is Paying Nicely for Company and Workers, Work and People, Vol: 15, Issue: 1, July 1994 pages 6-7

12. Anonymous. Japan to the Rescue, German Brief, Vol: 6, Issue: 18, May 6 1994, pages 4-5

13. Owen, Jean V. & Epram, Eugene E., Shop Floor '94: The Power

of Partnerships, Manufacturing Engineering , Vol: 112, Issue: 4, April 1994, pages 33-42

14. Cosco, Joseph, Service with a Smile, Journal of Business Strategy, Vol: 15, Issue: 2 March/April 1994, pages 58-60

15. Markowich, M. Michael, Does Money Motivate? Compensation and Benefits Review, Vol: 25, Issue: 1, January/February 1994, pages 69-72

16. Markowich, M. Michael, Is your Company's Revenue Greater than it's Expenses? HR Focus.Vol: 71, Issue:1 January 1994, pages 4-6

17. Tracey, John A., Profit Dynamics, Dow Jones-Irwin, Homewood, Illinois 60430, 1989

18. Welsh, Glenn A., Budgeting: Profit Planning and Control, Englewood Cliffs, NJ, Prentice-Hall, 1988, 4th edition

19. Dick-Larkam, Richard, Profit Improvement Techniques: an Action Programme for Management. Epping, Essex, Gower Press, 1973

20. Lines, James, Profit Improvement: a comprehensive approach to improving managerial effectiveness, London, Business Books, 1973

21. Senju, Shizno, Profitability analysis: Japanese Approach, Tokyo, Asian Productivity Organisation, 1989

Improving sales

Make it fun to shop

Make your store interesting, so that customers enjoy being there

Make your store interesting, so that one of your customers sitting at home with nothing to do might think, 'I'll just go down the road to such and such store. There's always something going on and I enjoy having a look around - it's fun.' If you can make your retailing entertaining, you are well on the road to having an extremely successful retail operation. This demands from you a total customer orientation. And you must enthuse every one of your staff with the same energy and commitment to serve.

Enjoy yourself

Follow the advice offered here. There is little that you will not have heard before, and little that you do not already know. There are no new retailing tricks. It is a matter of doing it – establishing the discipline in your store and enjoying the success resulting from that discipline.

Make your work fun. Enjoy the act of working, which requires a positive attitude from you. Begin with better management of yourself and your attitudes. Exhibit disciplined, energetic good humour, and lead your staff to retailing success.

Be responsive to your customers

Talk to your customers

The best way to find out what your customers want and like is to ask them. One option is focus groups, using 10 to 15 customers whom you know reasonably well and can invite to participate in a discussion. Other techniques for uncovering your customer wants and preferences include a service questionnaire handed out with every order, or regular customer surveys of, say, eight to ten percent of the people shopping in the store, or simply making sure that you spend time on the shop floor so that you can see how your customers and staff interact. Observe your customers' reaction to the various departments, get to know some of them, stop and talk to them in the store, and find out what they enjoy and what they do not enjoy.

It is important to have both formal and informal feedback from your customers. Informal feedback is obtained by walking around your store, talking, watching and listening. Formal feedback, on the other hand, is structured reporting on your customers' needs and preferences. When soliciting formal feedback, particularly through a survey, it is worth employing a trained person to actually interview people coming in or going out of your store, using a prepared questionnaire to guide the interview. That way you have some control over the data you collect.

> Your staff are another source of information about your customers' needs and preferences, particularly those who interact with your customers on a regular basis. Ask them what they think about their departments, being sure to focus them on the areas where they are likely to have sufficient expertise for you to have confidence in their judgment - that is, discussing their department or section, rather than the marketing of the store as a whole.

Talk to your customers, and keep talking to them.

Get to know your regular customers

Encourage your regulars by getting to know their names. Encourage your staff to do likewise.

This is more difficult than it looks. It takes concentration. Get your staff to practise remembering names and putting names to faces. Run short training sessions using photographs of people with their names underneath and asking staff to recall the name when a photograph is shown for the second time. Also encourage your staff to use the names that are available to them - for example, on a credit card or a cheque. Train them to read the name, then look up and address the person by name. The virtue of being able to call your customers by name is well understood. The difficulty is committing the time, the patience, and the effort to make sure it happens in your store - and happens regularly.

Keep records and use direct mail

The computer makes marketing activities possible that were unthinkable merely a few years ago. For instance, if you sell children's shoes, be sure to get the birth date of every child who buys shoes in your store, put the information in your computer, then on each child's birthday send the parent a reminder that the child is now a year older and will need new shoes. If you sell paintings, or fancy crockery, or ordinary crockery, or clothes, or almost anything, for that matter, when you get in a new line of goods send a leaflet on it to people who might be interested. This, of course, will entail keeping records on who is interested in what. An extremely successful women's dress shop uses this marketing technique almost exclusively. The proprietor works very hard at coming to know and understand the tastes and preferences of her clientele. When she sees a garment in a supplier's range that would suit a particular customer, she sends that customer a letter describing the garment and encouraging the customer to come in and try it on and have a cup of coffee at the same time. It is a very powerful marketing technique.

The concept is simple enough. The benefits are obvious. Do it now.

Become a local identity

Make yourself part of the community. The way you do this will depend on your personality, your skills, and something that could be called your pizzazz. A local supermarket manager in a country town successfully outsold a large chain merely by becoming a local identity. On the radio, and in local shows and celebrations, he was always to the fore, talking, getting to know people, and having fun with the community, and people responded by purchasing their food in his store. If you feel unable to behave like that, you should at least belong to some local clubs. Become involved in something somewhere. Alternatively, encourage some of your key staff to undertake the role for you. This will almost certainly involve paying for their club subscriptions and giving them time off if, for instance, they are going to manage the local cricket club or football club.

In my home town, both the Mad Butcher's retail meat shops and the Cycle Warehouse have been promoted by individuals prepared to make themselves local characters. As a technique, it works.

Review your products frequently

Keeping in touch with your customers' changing preferences is one part of the problem. The other is to keep in touch with the new products available. You should regularly review the range of products offered by all your suppliers, and also review any new suppliers. Work harder at improving the match between what your customers want and the products available in your store.

Match the style of your store to the style of your customers

A chain of low-cost men's and boy's clothes stores decided to upgrade their image. They redecorated, they moved their product range significantly up-market, resulting in higher prices, and in several instances, they relocated their stores to more prestigious suburbs. On the face of it, they were matching product and potential customers. It didn't work. The staff in the stores had not changed – they were used to dealing with straightforward family people. The up-market boutique customer they found much more difficult. The habits and the style of the staff did not fit. Within 18 months the chain reverted, simply because its new image had failed to hold enough of its old customers and failed to attract enough new ones. In a similar way, a chain of women's clothes stores offering a wide range, not fitted to any particular niche, flourished in good times but in bad times found it had no particular client or customer base. It had no loyal supporters, people who always shopped there. As a result, in a recession, it had to close.

Matching your store to your customers is not just a matter of redecorating and putting in goods aimed at customers you think are out there. Take stock of the existing customers; mould and develop and innovate your product line in relation to what they want and need now. Build on what you have. And, while doing that, establish a uniqueness about what you have to offer, so that those customers will come back to your store whenever they want to buy that type of product. Matching your store to your customers is an ongoing process. You need to listen to your customers and listen to any new or potential suppliers. Then, from all the data you have gathered, you need to make the blend. Be careful, however, not to unsettle those customers who shop in your store now.

Move with great care, one cautious step at a time.

Test, test, test

Test all aspects of your store's operation. Talk to customers and discover what layout of the store they would find most advantageous. Then reflect carefully on what you think would be most advantageous for the store. Shift a department from position A to position B and see if you achieve more sales. Don't shift everything all at once necessarily. Shift a department or two departments at a time. Swap them and observe the effect. Watch carefully what your customers buy. What sorts of things are the major selling lines? Make sure that these are given a high profile and good display positions in your store. Experiment by placing strong displays in different positions to see which are the most effective. Which produce the most impulse buying? Which give the longest selling time?

When thinking of introducing a new product or a new product range in your store, put it on trial first. Place the product in a position you think appropriate, give it a suitable display, then carefully measure the results. Use questionnaires and focus groups and discussions with your customers to see what they think of the new line. Will it suit the store, and will it suit their needs? Test, test, test. Managing your store involves more than administration or leadership. It also involves creativity in establishing what is the best stock, presentation and layout. This matching act requires intense experimentation. The end results are better sales and a more profitable store.

Give good value

Work hard at ensuring that your customers get the value for money they expect. If you operate an economy store, then be sure that your service is friendly, the goods are sound value for money, and your premises are not pretentious. If you operate an up-market store, catering for people who do not mind spending an extra pound, then be sure that the service matches, the premises match, and the atmosphere and ambience match. Maintain your quality – that is, the quality of the whole package that is your store (a combination of product, service, ambience, energy, excitement and image). If you operate a roadside restaurant offering primarily steak and chips and salad, then make sure that your chips are not greasy or your salad wilted. If you operate an economy clothes store, be sure that your price tickets are not dog-eared, your displays tired-looking, or your racks untidy. Quality and value for money are equally important at the upper and lower ends of the market.

Build repeat business through value and service

Value and service are not accidental. To review yours, make a list of every aspect of the service in your store. Start with product range, pricing, ticketing, store layout, availability of staff, cheque and credit facilities, checkout arrangements, and any other items that improve the service of your store. Then, for each item of service, write down the typical standard that your store achieves. Then write down an improved standard. Then begin increasing the standards in your store until they reach the new improved standards. Do all this without spending money, merely upgrading the quality of what you do now. Do the same for value, and value for money. Work at it, then work at it some more until you get it right. Then, once you have it right, create a new standard and start the practice again. Your sales and profits will benefit.

Know what you are best at

Keep in mind the mission, or theme, of your store. If you are at the economy end of the market, then make that clear. Stock sound, well-made goods at very competitive prices. If, on the other hand, you are at the upper end of the market, be clear about what you are offering. If it is a high-class men's clothes store, catering for the businessmen, then your mission is to turn out the best-dressed businessmen. Elegance, taste, understatement, good-quality cloth, style, fashion, and name brands will all be important. Be clear in your mind about the niche and the mission of your store. What, precisely, are you trying to do? You should write it down and be able to describe it and discuss it with your staff. This is what you and your staff will be best at; this is what you will be proud of.

Ensure that your staff know what the store is best at

Having worked it out in your mind, having established the mission and targeted the market niche, then make it clear to your staff what the store is to be best at. Work on the premise that everyone wants to be more proud of what they do than they are now.

Promote the theme to your staff. We offer the best deal, we dress the best businessmen, we offer the best service, we offer the most fashionable product, we offer the freshest goods – whatever it is, promote it-to your people.

It is important that your people don't merely do their jobs; they should become involved with the store's mission. As a result, far more of your human resources will be committed to achieving the high-quality, effective retail outlet that you seek.

Never compromise in giving value to customers

Beware of compromises, particularly those that may affect the customer. Maintain your standards at the highest level. This necessitates knowing what those standards are. If you do not know, think about them today and establish them clearly in your mind. Then insist on them at all times. Specify which of your staff need to know which of the systems and procedures. Then run a course bringing everybody up to the necessary standard of performance.

Run regular retail-selling workshops. The basic retail-selling skills may be taught in a three- or four-day course, conducted within your organisation or by an outside training company. In addition to this, at staff meetings or special meetings, you should discuss how to sell particular products. Get your experienced salespeople to share their ideas. Try bringing everybody up to an improved standard.

There should be sufficient product knowledge training to equip all your salespeople with the basic knowledge necessary to enable them to answer customers' queries. The key to successful selling is to establish in the mind of the customer confidence in the product, the company and the salesperson. Weak or inappropriate product knowledge will not achieve this. Use suppliers to run product knowledge sessions during lunch-times, evenings or tea breaks. Use the expertise in the store, people who are most familiar with the product, to train other staff up to a lesser but adequate standard. In addition to this practical and dedicated training, try to reshape and mould the attitudes in your store.

You are looking for constant innovation, creativity, and ways to improve the presentation of the store and products. Use your training to facilitate and aid this process.

Build a coherent store image

Use good layout and fixtures appropriate to the product

There is nothing worse than seeking a product in a retail store and struggling against poorly laid-out goods and badly designed fixtures, such as a bin where all the goods are jumbled up together in different sizes, colours or styles. At the start of the day the bin might have been organised, but by the time three customers have rummaged through it the contents are totally disorganised and will take hours for the poor staff member to sort out. Get better fixtures.

View the display from the customer's point of view

This is perhaps the hardest thing of all. Go into a department as if you are a customer going in for the very first time. Go with the intention of buying a particular item, and see what happens to your orderly stacks. See how long it takes to mix them up and make items difficult to find. Test. If there is any problem at all, any hint of frustration, then immediately seek ways of being more creative, so that the customer is given greater access, more effective access, and easier access.

Avoid empty spaces

Empty spaces create a negative effect on the customer. Use the space for a similar line, or the same line in a different size, or fill if with another product altogether. If all else fails, place a sign in the space explaining that the product is out of stock, why it is out of stock, and when it will be back in stock.

Place associated products close to good sellers

Place belts with trousers, bottle openers with bottles, ties with shirts, costume jewellery with dresses, and so on. Be more creative than you are being now. Again, take a blank piece of paper, write down all your major sellers and where they are located, and then list all of the items that could be associated with them. Use brainstorming as your major creative tool. Then, once you have made your list, reflect on it and select those items that seem to be most appropriate or that best enhance your store's image and don't make it appear too cluttered.

Change displays regularly

To keep your store alive and interesting, be sure to change your displays on a regular basis, even if, as in car selling, you are merely rotating your stock around the yard or around the store. This will attract people's attention and interest again; they may see something they didn't see last time they passed or last time they were in your store. Change displays frequently to attract more attention than you are getting now.

Be creative and appealing

Be more creative. Work harder at it, and do not lose your focus – concentrate your creative efforts on moving the product from your store to the customer, while at the same time being supported by tight, efficient and well-constructed systems and procedures that protect the profit potential of that product. Retailing is not a passive act. It is an exciting, vigorous, fun activity requiring tight discipline in order to protect the profit. Work on your creativity. Your store and your profits will benefit.

Balance space against profitability

The objective is to be profitable. High-volume lines require space in order to save on the expense associated with the repetitive shelf-filling necessary if the space they are allocated is too small. But that line may not be the best profit contributor to the store. So place the high-volume line low down; give if 80 percent of the space it might otherwise have allocated to it. Then place a less popular line that sells in lower volumes but produces a much better gross profit at eye level. The intention is to influence the customer with no strong preference, encouraging them to buy the less well-known brand, at the same price, giving you a better gross profit. Review your whole store with this in mind.

Use displays to enhance store image

Good displays will move product and add to the overall energy of your store. Involve your staff in ideas for making your displays more imaginative, more eye-catching and more fun. Set up a store committee that reviews and plans the weekly displays. You don't have to depend on your own creativity; good managers see that things get done and don't always do things themselves.

Know the store atmosphere you want

First, select five or six words that describe the store atmosphere you are seeking. Then review your store and see if it lives up to those words. Better still, ask someone you trust to review your list, walk into the store, and give you feedback about whether or not the atmosphere you seek is indeed evident. Be sure that the image you seek matches the perception of your customers. Ask them. Share with them the image you are striving to achieve and get their reactions to it. Use a focus group, or a survey, or merely stop three customers in your store whom you know and talk to them.

When seeking comments from customers, bear in mind that if you have a lot of displays and promotions in your store, a customer is likely to say that it is too cluttered and that they would like an easier place to shop. However, if you took away all the promotions and displays, the same customer would probably say that your store is dead and they would like more energy and excitement. So, when listening to your customers, do so with good judgment and good sense. Balance what they say and seek a rounded view based on your experience and judgment as a store operator.

Think of ideas for improving store presentation

Once you have settled on five or six words that describe the atmosphere you are seeking to create in your store, take each word, write it on a blank piece of paper, then write down five or six ideas for improving store presentation relating to that word. For example, energy may be a word that you have chosen. Ideas relating to that word could include more promotions, more creative displays, more vigour exhibited by staff, and more in-store demonstrations. Do the same for the other words on your list. Measure your store against the atmosphere you seek, then create additional ideas for improving on it. Involve your staff in this process.

Mould the store to the wants and needs of your customers

Store image and atmosphere, merchandising and product presentation, staff attitudes, product knowledge and selling skills - all contribute to the overall impact of your store on the customer. They are all separate and clearly identifiable areas that with creativity and effort can be improved and upgraded. It is doubtful that there is any single major thing to do in your store that would dramatically affect sales or profits. If it was anything that obvious, you would have seen it and dealt with it by now. Rather, the process is one of gradual improvement – a focused, determined effort in each of these areas, one at a time. Often, some of the efforts may not seem to be having a great deal of effect, but you are now dealing with small improvements that over a year or two years could easily increase the sales and profits in your store by 50 or 60 percent. So it may take several years for the results to be reflected in store performance – it may take that long for the appropriate behaviour to become a habit among you and your team.

Strengthen in-store selling

Congratulate staff when sales targets are achieved

Be enthusiastic about the results and efforts of your salespeople. Always be prepared to go up, shake someone's hand, and say thank you for a job well done. Make this the standard manner in which your people relate to one another. Encourage them to be pleased when somebody exceeds a goal, and be sure that everybody in the store congratulates that person. Departments that do well should be acknowledged at weekly branch meetings or at a lunchtime meeting called for that purpose. Recognise the people who do well. By rewarding good behaviour, you will increase the likelihood of such behaviour being repeated.

Set sales goals that staff can immediately understand

Sales goals should be broken down and made relevant to the actual behaviour of the salesperson in the store. For instance, a large supermarket sought a ten percent increase in the store's gross profit. In breaking down the sales needed to achieve such a goal, it came down to 45 pence extra on every sale made. Each department then analysed what sales increase it thought it could achieve and how it could be achieved. The net result of the drive was a 65 pence increase in the store's average sale. The point, of course, is that most salespeople in the supermarket could not relate to a 10 percent increase in gross profit, but could relate to gaining an extra 60p from every sale they made.

The same principle applies to any store. People should know what the average sale is, and if a sales increase is sought, they should know what percentage increase of the average sale that represents and also the increase in pound value that it represents. Then they can brainstorm ways and means of achieving the increase and understand it in relation to their own behaviour.

Ensure that staff maximise every sale

Your sales staff should be trained to maximise every sale. Any resistance is usually because they do not wish to be 'pushy'. Guide your sales staff merely to ask questions like: 'Would you like a shirt, sir? Would you like a tie, socks, handkerchief, or a belt, perhaps?' Or, if selling paintings: 'This small one would complement the large one you have just bought.' Or, at the very least, suggest that they say: 'We are expecting some more paintings in three months that are very similar to this, and by the same artist; perhaps you would like to come to our showing?' As part of your regular training, get your staff to look at all the extra products that could be sold in conjunction with the main product lines. If they think it out in advance, they are more likely to do it. Practice will help make the behaviour a habit, so practise in your department meetings. Get your staff in role-play making add-on sales. Your profits will benefit.

Insist on good standards of cleanliness and product presentation

The store should be clean and tidy, with all the products well presented. Understand the difference between presentation and merchandising. Presentation is to do with being clean, effective and efficient.

Merchandising adds the creative element and makes your presentation eye-catching and appealing, increasing the sale of the product. Merchandising causes people to stop in their tracks.

List every area of cleanliness in your store. Write down the standard that is typically achieved now, and write down a new improved standard. Then start at the top, and work through every standard until you have increased the overall performance of your store. This is basic.

Encourage sales by merchandising

There are two types of purchase – planned and impulse. Some would argue that impulse purchasing can be as much as 70 percent of all retail purchases. So you should know where the hot spots and the dead corners are in your store. Which areas move product best? In those areas you should put popular goods with a high gross profit. Your product presentation should be clear, tidy, easily appreciated, appealing, and well ticketed. Your store should also be laid out logically and sensibly so that new people coming into the store can find their way about it easily. Your merchandising should then be added on top of this basic presentation level; it should be eye-catching, interesting, tempting and above all creative. Your merchandising should be backed up by product presentation, demonstrations, and the energy and excitement of people enjoying what they do. The bulk of your product will be located in the primary positions in your store, with the secondary positions – such as bins and ends – being used for promotions and displays.

The key elements in merchandising include layout, making the best use of the flow of customers, and fixtures and fittings – having the correct shelving (with books on sloping shelves and children's underwear in well-labelled bins of a similar size and colour to avoid the customer having to ferret about in a jumble of sizes, colours, brands and styles). The store should have good lighting and a clean smell. Maintain cleanliness and a tidy floor. Use appropriate music to create a good atmosphere. Avoid obvious out-of-stocks. Keep up the store's energy and activity level with promotions and displays. Above all, you should build on the benefits of the products, not just the features.

Remember that eye level is sales level, and ensure that in your primary locations are the goods you want to move, arranged in vertical displays, not horizontal displays. The speed of sales should be balanced against gross profit – that is, give the best space to the product with the best gross profit, even if it does not sell the largest volumes. To avoid repetitive filling of shelves, make sure that fast-moving products have sufficient shelf space. All space should be filled; around your primary location there should be associated items – for example, bottle openers with bottles or belts with trousers. And beware of price tickets; large price tickets in the front may hide goods at the rear, especially if the goods are displayed flat. Build eye-catching displays, with contrasting colours or something unusual, such as a pig's head in a delicatessen. And do not make your displays too symmetrical; it is better to have something that disturbs the eye. In your merchandising, look for gaps and opportunities in the local market. Are there any minority groups? What specialist products may they demand? What could be displayed effectively? Such a display would attract them into the store and encourage them to purchase more in your store. Make it a fun atmosphere, make buying enjoyable, thank the customers and entertain them.

Improving store promotion

When promoting your store, know where your customers come from

Typically, a retail store – particularly one in the suburbs – draws its clientele from the area in which it is located. Inner-city stores tend to draw from a wider geographical area and depend on passing foot traffic. Often the clientele will include people who work in the surrounding offices.

Find out where you draw your clientele from. Work creatively on how to make contact and communicate with them. If you draw from the offices surrounding your store, see if you can arrange mail drops and direct mail shots into those offices. If you depend on passing pedestrian traffic, use billboards and strong window displays to attract attention. If you are a suburban store, arrange for advertising in your local suburban newspaper, or mail drops to the houses surrounding your store. Get to know your customers – what they read, what they like to wear, where they come from, and how you can make regular and better contact with them to promote your store and products.

Target your advertising

It has been said that half of all advertising is wasted – the problem is finding out which half. Today, that adage probably no longer applies. It is possible, by careful targeting, and by carefully following up the responses to your advertising, to establish which advertising works for you and which does not. Your research should not cost you a fortune. Be observant, talk to your customers, and talk to your friends, some of whom may be customers or potential customers, about what they read, what they enjoy reading, and what advertising they notice and respond to.

Do in-store surveys of your customers, asking question on what magazines they read, what television programmes they view, what type of travel they enjoy, and what form of transport they use. Then select from that the magazines most likely to have an impact on your customers.

For a local, suburban retail store, target your local paper, and don't forget involvement with local clubs and the local community – like the panelbeater who recently donated a Christmas tree, a 5 metre, living conifer, to be planted in the roundabout in the middle of his local shopping centre. This was an effective way of raising his profile in the community. And don't forget to involve your people in any good ideas. Encourage them to talk to their friends about the store and what the store has to offer. Recruit as an effective outside salesperson every member of your staff. For in the end, after all the advertising is done, your word-of-mouth promotion among your customers is your greatest asset.

Ask your customers why they come to your store

Every two or three months, do an in-store survey, identifying all new customers in your store and asking them why they came to your store, what attracted them to your store, what they liked and disliked about your store, and how they found out about your store. From this information, renew and refocus your advertising campaign, focusing at least some aspect of it on gaining new customers.

If you are a small- to medium-sized retailer, then do this every six months, remembering that it does not have to be a major event. Seek low-cost, low-key, focused solutions to the problems you face, one of those problems being simply gaining more clientele for your store. Increase your clientele, increase your sales and hence increase your profits.

Know your competitors' pricing and be prepared to compete

If your direct competitor is offering a similar product or a similar service in a similar type of store at a price lower than yours, then eventually your customers will go to the competitor.

Avoid direct price wars. Have a careful look at all you offer. Improve your service, improve your delivery, improve your lead time, improve your range of goods, improve the quality of your goods, improve your credit facilities, improve your direct marketing service – adopt some or all of these measures and any others you can think of in order to improve the package you offer. By improving the overall package, and not just the goods that people purchase, you can avoid competing merely on price. People pay the extra if they feel they are getting the extra service. Value for money is not merely the price of the goods; it is the service, the support, the friendliness, and the whole package that is your store. Work harder with your people and get it right. Be more creative. Review all your standards, and constantly improve them, so that you offer something better than the opposition, not merely a better price.

Remember that your reputation is the best advertising

While searching for new customers, don't forget the old ones. Be sure that your staff remember the names of your regular customers, and that you have mailing lists of your regular customers, indicating what they buy, so that you can focus direct marketing on them. Retaining an old customer is far cheaper than recruiting a new one.

Protection of store gross profit

Establish daily routines

Encourage discipline in staff

The best form of discipline is self-discipline. Consider now how you could encourage more self-discipline in your staff. First, tell them. Self-discipline is another expectation you have of their performance at work; if you don't tell them you have that expectation, they are less likely to exhibit it. Talk to key members of your staff about how they would like you to manage. What sort of tone or climate should exist in the team, and how is that best achieved? Building up self-discipline takes time. It follows that, in situations where there is insufficient time, the manager must direct people. But it is important that you only direct people when the conditions really demand it. Ensure that your actively taking responsibility for discipline is necessary and not just a matter of habit. When one of your employees fails to exhibit the necessary self-discipline, say that you are disappointed, that you feel let down, and then ask the employee what he or she proposes to do about that. If the response is flippant, or suggests that the employee is unlikely to develop the self-discipline you seek, then you must firmly discuss your expectations and confront the employee about whether he or she will ever endeavour to live up to them.

The discipline of systems or procedures provides the framework that protects the existing profit potential. On top of this framework must be added the service and merchandising elements that create the dynamic experience of your retail store. These too require discipline – to handle staff, attract attention, and generate energy and excitement for your customers. By encouraging your staff to exercise self-discipline, you will help them to gain satisfaction from a deeper and fuller involvement with the key factors that underline the success of the store.

Communicate simply and directly

Communication is another discipline. There are no new things to learn; it is merely the careful, effective implementation of the things we already know.

- Ask employees for their ideas and opinions, then select the best and be sure to implement them.
- Listen more and talk less.
- Maintain direct eye contact while listening or speaking.
- Explain the reasons for doing things.
- Show employees respect and talk as one adult to another, speak from the heart, not from the head or from some notion of how a manager should speak.
- Make sure your employees understand what you expect from them.
- Give instructions and assignments clearly, so there will be no misunderstandings.
- Consider employees' feelings by trying to see things from their viewpoint.
- Stay calm and collected, particularly under pressure.
- Make the best use of people and resources to get the job done.
- Plan and organise every day, follow up every day, and be prepared to revise your plan every day in the light of new circumstances.
- Delegate tasks easily.
- Motivate employees by showing them how they can be more successful at what they do, by guiding them in their self-disciplined involvement with their job.
- Co-operate and insist on co-operation. But at all times communicate your energy and zest for the direction in which you are taking the store, and the excitement you feel about the achievement of this week's goals and this week's plans for realising these goals.

Have a plan for every day

Each day you should know what you are going to do that day. But do not hold rigidly to that plan. When you arrive in the morning, check your plan against any emergencies that may have occurred. If the priorities you felt were important the night before are still appropriate, then carry out your plan. If not, then adjust your plan in light of the new factors and new priorities. This process should take from 15 minutes to half an hour, and should be the first thing you do almost every morning. When you come in, open up, speak to any employees who may be present, go to your office, and review your plan. This is a simple daily routine, guiding you into the discipline that you will need to exhibit for the rest of the day.

Your daily goals should be behavioural – that is, they should specify clearly the actions you propose to take that day. These daily actions should add up at the end of each month to the achievement of your monthly goals. Hence, once per month, you should spend an hour or two examining what you propose to achieve during the next month, then breaking that down into your weekly goals, which in turn are broken down into your daily tasks and priorities.

Your monthly goals must obviously be derived from your annual goals. It follows that every year you should spend several days planning your budgets and overall goals for the store for the coming year. And your annual goals should be derived from your overall vision of the business. What sort of store are you developing7 This planning process is simple, clear, and well understood by virtually all managers. There is nothing new involved. It is another discipline – one that is essential to your success.

Guide your staff in their daily priorities

For every department in your store, or every section, you should have a routine card. This routine card should remind the staff members or department head or section leader what must be done in that department on a daily or weekly basis. It should include things like stock recovery, facing up, cleanliness, ticketing, refilling of shelves, and any other regular and repetitive task that needs completing in the department. Maintenance of this routine should ensure that the department meets the standards you require.

Once this basic routine is in place, the staff can then begin to concentrate on the merchandising and overall presentation of their department or section. Building on the basic layout and cleanliness established by the routine, they can create eye-catching displays or look at other layout factors that may contribute to catching the customer's eye or drawing more customers into the department or section. Where appropriate, the department head or section leader should have weekly meetings with their staff in their department or section, reviewing the routine, discussing how it can be improved, and examining any other tasks that need to be completed or ways in which the section or department can be upgraded. In a similar way, you, as branch manager or store manager, could have meetings with your department heads or section leaders, reviewing with them the same sorts of factors.

Allow for the unexpected

No plan can be rigidly adhered to. Any manager who produces a weekly plan and follows it religiously is simply not relating to what is going on around him or her. New issues and problems will arise that need to be considered or absorbed into the existing plan. Unexpected things will happen. Often new opportunities will occur, such as a supplier's sales representative walking in with a new promotion or a presentation idea, or a local radio station deciding to launch a particular product in a particular way, and you can capitalise on the opportunity by doing something in your store. It is essential to plan, but your plans must never become rigid frameworks preventing you from correcting problems or causing you to miss creative opportunities for maximising the performance of your store.

Establish strong store routines

Set the standard for your store by ensuring that you have strong routines yourself. What tasks need doing every day? Every week? Re-examine the detailed checklist for every task in your store. Are all of those items 'embedded' in store systems? Do your staff know what to do, when to do it, and how to do it? Create a daily diary for yourself. It should involve checking every department every day. It should allow time for sales representatives. It should have on it the basic weekly tasks of invoicing, reports, stock ordering, and any other regular tasks in your store. Make a list of these daily and weekly tasks, put them into a routine, then keep to your routine. It is another discipline. Avoid disrupting your routine.

The unexpected will always occur, and you need to be ready for it, but do not allow it to dominate your routine. Bend your routine to the unexpected, and fit the unexpected into your routine. For instance, the sales representative of an important supplier from out of town appears unannounced at a time when you have not allowed for a meeting. Meet with the representative for a few minutes and negotiate a time for a second, longer meeting. Or, if your routine will allow it, see the representative immediately, but discuss how such problems can be avoided in the future.

Maybe one of your employees comes to you seeking a meeting when you are in the middle of drawing up an important schedule for a supplier – negotiate a time with the staff member, so that you can complete the schedule while your mind is on it and devote your attention to the employee when you meet. Seek to keep to the discipline of your routine.

Once your own routine is working, encourage, through the use of routine words, all of your staff to do the same.

Ensure that staff understand and follow store routines

Systems and procedures provide the discipline that protects the store's profit potential. Be sure that every member of your staff understands this basic concept. If necessary, have short training sessions at lunch-times or after work, discussing this idea until your people understand fully why it is so important. Once they understand the concept, get them to apply it tightly to your store, This will encourage them to identify behaviour that is consistent with the concept and behaviour that is not.

For instance, in the analysis of inward goods through the storeroom, behaviour that does not involve checking all goods carefully against packing slips is clearly inconsistent with the principle. Similarly, failing to record markdowns or returns is also inconsistent with the principle. It is worth examining, with your staff, every type of behaviour that is consistent with the principle and every type of behaviour that is inconsistent with it. Having done this with all your employees, and with every new one to arrive, and having had a refresher session every three or four months, then you should confront any staff members whose attitude remains inconsistent with the principle. Such people will undermine the potential performance of your store. If they are unwilling or unable to adopt the appropriate attitude, then you will need to reconsider whether they should remain members of your staff.

Maintain tight store controls

Know that systems protect profit and store atmosphere makes sales

Adopt this concept as the underlying premise of everything you do in your store. Systems and store atmosphere are the two main factors that will determine your success. The two other factors are having your goods at competitive prices and having your store located in a suitable position.

The key success factors can be summarised as follows:

- **Systems and procedures**
- **Store atmosphere and shopping experience**
- **Product range and quality**
- **Store location**

Price is included as part of store atmosphere and shopping experience, while product quality incorporates value for money. Use these concepts to focus your efforts. Concentrate on those variables that are most likely to give you a good return for your efforts.

Tightly control factors likely to erode the store's margins

Unknown shrinkage is a major factor contributing to inadequate store profits. Unknown shrinkage arises in a number of ways including:

- pilfering by staff
- shoplifting
- breakages in the store
- unrecorded discounts
- goods on a packing slip not received physically
- unrecorded defective goods
- returned goods and refunded sales where the goods are not returned to stock
- inaccurate stock-taking.

As you can see, only two of these items relate to theft. The others all relate to systems and procedures in the store that ensure that all movement of goods is recorded accurately. It is essential that these factors are tightly controlled.

Educate staff on the importance of these disciplines

Berating staff who fail to obey the disciplines laid down in the policies and procedures manual will not work in the long run. It is essential that they understand and that they think, for situations will arise every day in your store that cannot be detailed in a policies and procedures manual. Your staff must think about what they are doing. This means that they must understand the basis of how to make a retail store profitable. Talk to them about the philosophy that is behind the systems and explain that discipline protects the profit while the store atmosphere makes the sale. Talk to them about what the systems are, how they can be improved, where the errors occur, and what can be done about those errors. Make them understand the importance of filling in that stock check form, or that returned goods form, or counting every item on a pallet and making sure that it tallies accurately with the packing slip.

Praise them when they are doing these things properly. Help them maintain these crucial disciplines – you know it's hard, and you know it gets boring, and you know you don't always feel like being disciplined, but it is your job to help them develop their self-discipline.

Improve purchasing and stock control

When purchasing, have a firm attitude towards negotiations

Good negotiation begins with your attitude. Be determined to get a good deal. Provide good information to your suppliers, in terms of your likely orders, dates required, and invoicing and payment details. Treat them as well as you can; they are an important part of your organisation, second only to customers. Nonetheless, you must always act in the best interests of your business, for it is their responsibility to act in the best interests of theirs.

Be sure that any margin lost through discount is recovered

Don't give away money without planning to get it back. If you give large discounts to attract attention and to attract people into your store, have a clear idea and a clearly formulated plan on how that lost income is to be recovered. The discount can be recovered in a number of ways:

- by slightly increasing the price of a number of goods
- by allowing for a discount margin in the gross profit of every product in the store
- by selling an extra quantity of a particularly profitable line associated with the loss leader.

Think of different ways it can be recovered, but be sure to recover it.

Maintain tight stock control

The key to good stock control is minimising out-of-stocks while also minimising capital committed to inventory. There is no simple solution. First, determine the stock level you regard as appropriate for your store – that is, the overall pound value of the inventory you are prepared or are able to carry. Then, bearing in mind your customer base and your overall store philosophy, establish your stockholding product by product, so that its value does not exceed your budgeted inventory level. You should undertake a full stock-take every six months. This should then be combined with a full set of accounts on a six-monthly basis. You should maintain a tight inventory profile. Do not allow yourself to become overstocked with any particular line or product. Carefully estimate any specials that you intend to offer, and arrange for stock appropriate to a minimum sales level, with the ability to quickly obtain more supplies if they become necessary.

Do not stock yourself up and have surplus stock on your hands. Be constantly auditing the inventory profile. Stocks that sit there for several months need reviewing quickly, and as part of your pricing policy be sure that the cost of unsold items is built in.

Be cautious with your stock. Do not allow yourself to be talked into more than you need. And, when assessing for stock-take purposes the value of the stock, be ruthless in undervaluing last year's stock. Do not inflate your profits by including the full value of stock that in reality is not fully realisable.

Do not let stock accumulate in the stockroom

Have a very tight goods-in goods-out system. Be sure that every item coming into the stockroom is accounted for and checked against a packing slip. Then ensure that your packing slips are checked carefully against your invoices. Tight control of this system will eliminate unknown shrinkage due to administrative errors. Be sure to audit your goods-in procedures regularly, at least monthly and preferably once per week. Ensure that the stockroom is kept clean, tidy and well ordered. One way to accumulate stock is to allow your stockroom to become untidy, so that goods become lost in the back corner or under a pile of boxes and rubbish. An untidy stockroom will also result in more breakages than necessary.

Write off stock early and build write-off into the initial pricing

Do not carry last season's stock into the new season unless you are sure it will indeed sell. Aim to eliminate all of a season's stock within the season. And allow for a certain write-off of unsold stock in your pricing. Thus, if you have 100 items, and you seriously think that the minimum sold will be 75, build the cost of the 100 into the 75. If that is not possible for competitive reasons, or your store is not perceived as being able to carry such margins (i.e., your customers will not pay the necessary prices), then you may be forced to purchase a smaller quantity and organise a backup supply if needed. Or, alternatively, arrange the goods on a sale-or-return basis.

Above all, face stock retention problems early rather than late. If you feel some stock is not going to sell, talk to your senior staff about what can be done, and do this early. Ensure that your product is sold and is not still sitting on your shelves four months after the season has ended and the new season's radically different designs have been introduced.

Put new lines on trial first

Wherever possible, aim to put a new line on trial before purchasing in volume – even if that trial merely involves discussing the product with your key customers or one of your focus groups. Any trial will assist in establishing the volume you can move, and the amount of stock you may or may not have on your hands at the end of the sales period. Maintain sales records of styles, prices and volumes, to guide future purchases. Do not depend on your memory. And do not necessarily depend on suppliers' information. Keep some sort of sales book, recording sales product by product, including style, price, volume, and any discounts that had to be given away in order to quit the remaining stock. Record any difficulties that were encountered such as repair problems or consumer resistance. Also record any queries about goods you are not holding, variations on lines or styles you have not previously stocked.

Be sure to use this sales informnation when planning your purchasing next year.

Always ask for a better deal

The first rule of negotiating is always ask for a better deal.

- Ask for a lower price or a higher discount.
- Ask for a better price in return for taking a higher volume.
- Ask for supplier support in stocking your shelves.

- Ask for supplier support in putting up displays.
- Ask for a shorter lead time.
- Ask for better credit terms.
- Ask for a training session on the product by the supplier's sales representative.
- Ask for sale or return.
- Ask for vendor refill.
- Ask for broken and damaged stock to be credited more quickly.

There is never any harm in asking. Put it onto the supplier to say no. Do not assume that you cannot get a better deal, for you probably can.

Buy shrewdly

Shrewd purchasing is a key factor in successful retailing. If you run a small- to medium-sized retail store, do not delegate this task. Or, if you do delegate, delegate only the administrative aspects. Make the decisions about what is to be purchased yourself. If you are in a large store, the chances are you will have buyers in charge of product lines. However, be sure to audit what the buyers intend to purchase, and keep a close eye on them.

Successful buying is the art of buying products that precisely match the needs, values and aspirations of your clientele. It is not a science, but a shrewd art. It requires good judgment, daring, and insight into the nature of your clientele. Before making any large purchases, stand in your store and watch the customers come and go, see what they purchase and how they dress and walk, listen to what they talk about – the magazines they read, the movies they have seen recently, or the theatres they have been to – and from all of this draw your conclusions about the nature of the average customer.

Once you have done that, ask yourself if the average customer in your store would be interested in a particular product at a particular price. If you are in any doubt, test carefully first.

Leadership

Be a go-getter

Be enthusiastic

Smile. The first sign of enthusiasm is a smile. Smile at your staff, for your staff are your customers. Create the tone and the mood and the energy in your staff, and they in turn will take care of the customers who purchase from your store. Move with energy. Move briskly and in a businesslike way, but move with awareness, so that you notice the piece of scrap paper on the floor, the crooked price ticket, and the substandard merchandising, and you notice when the routines in the storeroom are not being followed sufficiently tightly for you to be confident that all of the goods booked in did in fact come in. Be willing to give your staff a lift when they are feeling low; with brisk businesslike good humour and energy encourage your staff to adopt the standards they need. Teach them the philosophy of your store and the key factors of market, service, standards and routines. Begin by smiling more at your staff.

Inspire people

Everyone wants to be more proud of what they do than they are now. This is a simple viewpoint that is seldom wrong. Are you giving your people a reason to feel more proud of what they do? What is your store going to be best at? What reason do your people have for coming to work other than having to earn their daily living? If you are a grocery retailer, then seek to offer the best service in your area, or offer the best prices in your area, or the cleanest and most friendly store. If you sell men's or women's clothing, offer the best service or the best price. Find a uniqueness about your store that gives the customer some satisfaction, then use this to inspire your people.

Work with people

Encourage people. Make the standards and values of your store clear to your staff. Then have them adapt your ideas to their own behaviour to deliver the performance standards you require.

Identify their strengths and encourage them. Respect their feelings, but at the same time teach them to think for themselves.

Encourage them to think about the store, the routines and the standards, and to do what they can to achieve the necessary performance levels for you.

A disciplined approach can be adopted towards simple things such as timekeeping. But again it is important to consider how to apply the discipline. For instance, if your staff are sitting too long at morning and afternoon teas, perhaps walk in and say, 'Well, I really think we should be getting back to work, don't you?' Try to avoid being too heavy-handed about it.

When discussing the philosophies of the store, aim to be persuasive, in a way that causes people to reflect. Avoid lengthy argument and debate; instead adopt a quiet questioning manner that makes staff think about the store and their own performance in it. Be the boss, but be alongside them and with them at the same time. This is a difficult balance to achieve well. It requires careful thought by you in how to approach your people to achieve the result you want. Leadership is not something you do twice a day or three times a week. It exists in every interaction you have with your staff.

For instance, let us imagine that you are stressed for some reason; your child is in hospital, say, and as you are rushing out of the store you speak to one of your staff to delegate a task, but your manner causes offence. A slight of this kind may take 24 hours to work its way out of a person's system. Now let us assume it is 10 hours later, and you are still rushing because of the pressure, and you delegate another task to the same person or they approach you for some reason and again you speak in a way that causes offence. Now offence builds on offence, slight on slight, and it may take 36 or 48 hours for the ill feeling to wear off. Then 24 hours later ... The leadership you build depends on these small daily interactions. If they are going the same way as in this example, then you are creating a negative climate in your store. The tensions will slowly overcome performance. You must be aware of your behaviour in this way. Managing yourself, balancing discipline with persuasion and enthusiasm, will help to achieve the dynamic climate that will make your store a success.

Check the store every day

Check all the key items on your list every day. All other items should be checked in a routine way – daily, weekly, monthly or quarterly. It may only be checked when you do your stock-take twice a year. Whenever the item on a checklist should be checked, then check it.

Put in the extra effort

If it needs doing, do it now. Maintain that sense of urgency. Help yourself to maintain that urgency by having a daily plan; then by midday, if you have achieved only half of your plan, you should increase the pace. These self-imposed deadlines will ensure that you are a model for your people, leading by example and getting your job done with the necessary sense of urgency.

You should plan every day. And your plan should be based on the priorities that need to be achieved. This means that each month you should assess what your priorities are for that month and what key tasks must be achieved each week to ensure that those key priorities or goals are achieved. Then your daily plan should reflect this thinking. Many of your daily activities will also involve things that come up during the day or the week. Deal with those by fitting them into the priority list. If such tasks are urgent and need to be dealt with immediately, then do so.

Be there. There is no better way to exercise leadership than to be at work yourself. Staff will respect that and will respond positively to it. Every manager accumulates over time a list of tasks in the 'too-hard' category, tasks that get put off. Every month or six weeks, make a list of those tasks, then make that list your priority list for the week.

Get them done. Inevitably you will find that none of them was as hard as you thought. Thinking about them is usually worse than doing them. Have a regular routine and stick to that routine so that when you arrive in the morning, you know exactly what you are going to do. Often you will do the same thing every Wednesday morning, and so your day starts to take on a pattern and a flow.

Regular items, such as checking invoices, should be done at a particular point in your routine. This way you can ensure that these chores do in fact get done on a regular basis. Priorities, plans and routines – your business will benefit from these disciplines.

Think more and think harder

Success requires three things: focus, intensity, and the discipline to put in place the necessary behaviour arising from the first two.

Focus:

- What are the key priorities for your store?
- What do you propose to concentrate on in order to improve the profits of your store?
- What standards do you propose to improve in your store?
- How do you intend to improve service to your customers?
- What do you propose to do in order to gain more customers?
- What is the focus for you?

You cannot be casual about focus; it requires hard work. It must be felt. There must be an intensity about your analysis and your thinking, and following that, an intensity of commitment to realising the goals that arise from your thinking. Once you have completed the intense, focused thinking and you have committed yourself to the plan that has arisen, then implement it. The implementation should reflect the same intensity of commitment; people should feel that you are committed to achieving these goals. It should be evident in your behaviour.

As a rule, be sure that when you are at work you are 100 percent at work. Doing this on its own will considerably increase your intensity at work. Often, increasing your presence at work does not necessitate longer working days, but working the same number of hours with greater intensity. That is, allowing yourself fewer distractions, or allowing private or personal issues to intrude into your thinking less and less. This is a difficult discipline but one that can increase your work output considerably; in many instances it can actually reduce the number of hours you work.

Effective action follows effective thinking. Think carefully first, think with intensity and focus, then do it.

Work hard at establishing where to put your effort for best results

You have one goal – to make the store profitable. When a sports team has a goal to win, the question then is how will the team win, what tactics will be adopted? In the same way you must consider the tactics for making your store more profitable. There are two key areas of focus: systems and procedures within the store designed to protect the profit potential of the store; and establishing and maintaining the flow of customers in order to realise the profit potential that has been so carefully protected. From these fundamental priorities are deduced specific goals and tasks that need to be actioned. Do this analysis in your store and identify where to place your effort in order to realise the best results that you can.

Typically, there will be a number of goals that need actioning from both of the focused areas at once. Seldom if ever is a store in a position where it is getting an adequate flow of customers and only the systems and procedures need correcting. And seldom or never is the situation the reverse of that. So examine your store now.

- Are your systems and procedures as tight as they need to be or could usefully be?
- Do you have an adequate flow of customers?
- What would attract more customers? And how?

When considering trying to increase the customer base or customer flow of your store, be very cautious about apparent 'quick-fix' solutions. Advertising will not necessarily achieve the result. Be cautious about committing significant increases in expenditure to advertising; adopt a cautious trial-and-error approach. Follow the response of all your advertisements so that you learn what kind of advertising works best for you. Try different systems and procedures in your store. Try different merchandising techniques. Guide your staff to work at different approaches to customers and different service approaches. Record the results of everything you try. Then follow up and assess effectiveness. Slowly, over time, you will come to learn and understand what really works in your store. After several months, select the best ideas, put them in place and build upon them. Work at your store. Success is not a matter of chance.

Keep your energy up

Keep yourself motivated. But first understand the relationship between action and motivation: motivation follows action. Do not wait for inspiration. The people who waited for inspiration are still waiting. Reflect on the last time you did the lawns, or tidied the garage; you may not have particularly wanted to do it, but once you got started, once you got halfway into it perhaps, you found it wasn't so bad and the task was completed comfortably. Then, when you had finished, you looked back and said, 'Hmm, yes, that's a job well done.'

Start acting – motivation will follow. That's the way it is. Be conscious of your own habits of acting and thinking that may undermine your self-motivation. It requires self-discipline backed by an understanding that motivation follows action. Once you get started, you will feel fine. Then simply discipline yourself to get started and feel the motivation flow into the task and the activity.

You can assist your motivation and give it urgency by setting yourself deadlines, goals, tasks, standards and levels of achievement. It is important to set deadlines for yourself and commit yourself to them. You should feel uncomfortable or upset when your self-imposed deadlines are not met. Let your conscience push you a little. Use this process. In addition, tell other people in your company or your family when you set goals for yourself and when certain tasks will be done. This social commitment will also help push you and commit you to the deadlines you are setting for yourself. Push yourself a little in this way, and guide your team to do the same. If you are not prepared to put pressure on yourself, do not expect your team to put pressure on themselves.

Move at a measured pace

To act with urgency is not to be frenetic. Avoid the appearance of rushing from one task to the next. Avoid the appearance of being pushed by one urgent issue to the next urgent issue. If one of your staff rushes into your office with a problem, listen to it carefully and then assess whether it really is as urgent as they would have you think, assess it against the priorities that are in front of you already, and then calmly determine your course of action.

Walk through your store in a brisk and businesslike manner. If you see two staff members chatting unnecessarily, make a breezy comment that you hope they are not going to do that for too long. Pick up the scraps of paper and straighten the price ticket; do so with controlled and measured urgency, not with frenetic impatience. Seek to create the impression of urgency controlled. Show that there is time for the critical things, those simple fundamentals that can be so easily overlooked. Create the impression that, even though you are concentrating on what you are doing, you never lose sight of the broader issues that make your store a success.

Be a complete manager

Know your business

Research has shown that good retail managers are complete managers. They are good at handling people and at all aspects of basic management, including in-store technology, store-specific skills, product knowledge, and building a positive culture in their stores so that the shopper enjoys a high-quality shopping experience. Learn about your product.

* What are its main features, and what benefits flow from those features?
* Why should a customer buy the product – what's in it for the customer?

- What are the advantages of one type of product over another?
- Under what circumstances should a customer purchase product A instead of product B, which is of a similar nature?
- How and when should the customer use the product, and what are the limits to the use of the product?

This product understanding presupposes an understanding of the market for which the product is intended. So know your market.

- What sort of people shop in your store?
- Where do they come from?
- Are they local people?
- Do they travel from all over the city, the county or the country?
- And why do they come?
- What are they looking for?

If you don't know answers to these questions, why not ask your customers? Select 40 regular customers, then arrange for after-work discussions of 10 or so at a time. Plan the discussion, make the discussion focus on the product, the service, the quality of the store, and what they themselves are looking for when shopping in your store. Critically examine the store itself. Take off your blinkers. Try to see the store from a brand-new customer's point of view.

- What do you see?
- If you were a brand-new customer walking into your store, would you be enthused?
- Would the staff successfully sell you something?
- What was the first thing you saw as you walked through the door?
- Was it a pile of boxes, or a fine, eye-catching and appealing display?
- Is your store organised for ease of customer movement and customer access to the goods?
- Is your store laid out in a sensible sequence?
- Are the goods that need to be accessible in fact accessible?
- What makes your store different from other stores, thus requiring different staff skills?

- Do your people have those skills?
- Are you up to date with the latest store technology?

This does not mean that you must necessarily implement every new idea or technological advance that comes along. But you do need to be familiar with any in-store technological advances, for if you are not, you are likely to ignore factors that could give your competitors an edge. Scanning, computerised stock control, computerised goods-in and goods-out systems, computerised stockroom control, electronic payment systems, and computer store design and layout systems – all and more are available.

Are you familiar with them? You need to be. All the technology and basic management skills need to be blended with good people skills. Leadership will always remain the basis of good retail management. Layout, merchandising, store decoration, cleanliness and housekeeping, good price ticketing, readily accessible products, clearly marked service centres, and a flexible exit and payment system to cope with regular and peak demand are all essential factors in store design. They will all help the customer have that high-quality shopping experience and consequently will persuade the customer to return to the store. But without the smile, and without the quality interaction, these factors will not be sufficient. It is your people who give the store its final character, so your people must be one of your primary concerns, as manager. A good retail manager leads by example – not by going in and doing the job for them, but by getting on with the manager's job with vigour, energy and 'hustle'. Good managers have the know-how and the energy and direct their effort where it has maximum impact. Do you?

Adopt the characteristics of a good manager

Good managers are creative; they are entrepreneurially orientated. They are innovative to the point of stretching the limits of their authority. But they get results through their efforts. Without results, the creative manager becomes a nuisance. Without results, the central organisation should and will impose its own methods. If you operate your own retail store, then the failure of your creative efforts will lead eventually to the demise of your store. Effective store managers have great talents for developing and fully utilising their employees. They involve themselves with their employees while remaining sufficiently distant to retain their authority as manager. And they are go-getters. They use their knowledge of people, and their knowledge of store and product technology, to maximise their effectiveness, and they are constantly blending technology, product and market factors with leadership of their own people.

Good managers set high standards for themselves, their employees, and their stores and see that those standards are met. They are demanding, they know what they want, and they work very hard to achieve it. They show people how to achieve good results. That means they do a lot of background research, talking and thinking. They are constantly looking for ideas. You must understand that ideas are the very basis of effective retailing.

Effective managers tend to place high value on working their way up. They feel it was essential to their own success and is, if the right help is provided, essential to their employees' success. They tend to be wary of people coming in, shall we say, at the top. The essence of retailing is understanding its simplicity and doing the simple, basic things well on a very consistent basis.

The best way to learn this is from the bottom up. Reflect on your own behaviour. Ask your employees about your behaviour. How well does it compare with this profile of an effective store manager? Begin today to reconstruct your own behaviour, to make it more professional and closer to that which research has shown to be most effective.

Do not adopt bad habits

If you want to fail as a retail store manager, then all you need to do is adopt some or all of the following habits.

- Dominate and control your subordinates.
- Require obedience rather than initiative and creativity.
- Oppose and stifle new ideas or suggestions for change.
- Avoid making decisions that have any risk of failure.
- Place little value on employees' participation and involvement when decision-making and problem-solving.

- Don't listen to your staff.
- Take every opportunity to belittle your staff.
- Stay with established or past practices rather than testing or experimenting with alternatives.
- Be lethargic in the store.
- Always be behind; never have the invoices out when they are supposed to be.
- Never get your work done in time.
- Always be late.
- Take lots of time off.

This list is far from exhaustive. You may wish to add habits you know of to it.

Listen to your team

The hard part of listening is to stop thinking about what you are going to say next. It is an act of self-discipline. It is hard, but the subsequent increase in commitment and effort of your staff will make it worthwhile. Concentrate precisely on what people are saying to you. Be sure that you understand what they are saying before commenting, and in particular before passing any judgment. Avoid interrupting people. Use phrases such as, 'Now let me see if I've got this right' or 'Now, as I understand it, what you're saying is....'

Take more time to really hear what is being said. Ask more questions. Say to people, 'Is this what you mean?' Keep testing until they agree that what you said is what they meant.

Seek out the ideas of your staff. Ask them. Then be sure to implement some of what they tell you. Encourage everybody to come up with ideas about how their particular job could be improved. Then encourage them to implement those ideas. Steady, progressive, bottom-up improvement of your organisation will be more lasting and pervasive than many of the grand schemes pushed down the organisation by the general manager or managing director. Encourage people to think effectively and creatively about their particular job. Listen more. It's harder than it sounds. It requires you to manage your own thinking habits with the deliberate intention of paying more attention to what people tell you rather than what you think for yourself. Do this and the performance of your team will improve as a consequence.

Be firm but fair

What does it feel like to be on the receiving end of you? Would you like to be managed by you? Seek from people you trust some feedback about your own behaviour. Try to alter those aspects of your behaviour that cause people to reduce their commitment and motivation. Be more assertive about what you expect. In order to do this, however, you must know what you expect. Therefore, be clear in your own mind about the standards and tasks you expect for every job and every routine in your store. Then, once you have established what needs to be done, make sure that all of your staff understand and know what is expected of them – and to what standard tasks must be performed.

Once everybody knows what they are to do, be sure they have the skills, knowledge and tools to do it. When people know what to do, and they are equipped to do it, they should get on with it. If they do not do so, you must quietly but firmly express your disappointment. Ask them why they have not done it. Listen carefully, then judge whether to accept what they say.

Stress repeatedly the essential disciplines of retailing – namely, appropriate presentation, quality customer service, and adherence to the systems and procedures that will protect the store's profit potential. Be sure that your staff know how these disciplines are to be implemented in your store. All the detailed skills, technology, product knowledge, and interpersonal relations are blended and put to use in serving the customer. Quietly but firmly insist on these disciplines and the implementation of these disciplines. Never merely exhort your people for better performance. Show them how to achieve it. And, when in doubt yourself, talk to them, ask them questions, and listen carefully to their answers. Use the creative resources of your people, and build effective solutions to those everyday problems that you and your staff will undoubtedly encounter in building an excellent store.

Manage the team ethics

As manager, it is your responsibility to control how your staff act towards each other. For instance, do not allow internal feuds between staff members. Where a feud occurs, call both parties into your office, tell them they are working for a professional organisation and the performance of the team will not be allowed to suffer as a consequence of their personality conflict. Do not get them into your office to act as mediator or play some counselling role. It does not work. If the conflict is based on work factors, and not personality, then you may have to determine what the solution is to be and simply insist that it is now out of their control and they are to settle down and work co-operatively together. Stress also that they do not have to like one another; they merely have to respect one another and co-operate sensibly to the benefit of the team.

Do not discuss staff with other staff. Do not play favourites. At any one time there will be some staff in your company whom you will really enjoy working with and will be a delight to have around, and there will be other staff whom you do not enjoy working with, who are always creating difficulties, and who are not particularly nice to have around. The key to good leadership is that these people should not know your feelings towards them. All they should understand is your view of them as a participant in an effective and professional team, charged with the responsibility of achieving a commercial result. Where their behaviour is inconsistent with achieving a good result, they must be spoken to quietly and firmly. But your personal reaction towards them has no place in such discussions. Be clear and firm that staff must treat one another openly, honestly and non-defensively. This can be carried through to actually setting team goals, or encouraging the team to maintain pressure on one another to achieve those goals. Set the example in your team by conducting yourself with the highest ethical standards.

Set clear goals

Be sure that all staff members know what is expected of them. Reward and recognise employees who live up to your expectations and achieve their goals. Devise new ways of rewarding and recognising employees:

- wages and salary increases
- a dinner out with his or her partner
- a trip to Hawaii, Singapore, Paris or London
- a night out in a local hotel
- a simple thank you
- a simple thank you in front of all the other staff at a meal break
- a special certificate
- a notice posted on the notice board
- involvement in certain management functions
- a commendation from the board
- a half-day off
- some other special privilege unique to your store, allowing them to buy a certain product at a privileged discount
- a small gift
- a promotion.

By regularly consulting with them you exhibit through your behaviour a special trust that gives them a unique position in the store.

When setting goals for staff, be sure that the goals are in terms they can relate to and that they are specific. For instance, seeking a sales increase of 5 percent is quite inappropriate as a goal for retail sales staff in your store. It would be better, if the average sale were £45, to restate the goal as seeking an extra £2.25 per sale. In a clothing store, that might amount to selling a matching handkerchief. In a toy store it might amount to ensuring that batteries are sold with all the electronic toys. Work out what the pound increase in sales means in terms of each actual sale for your people. Then encourage them to think and develop those habits.

Your staff should also know their weekly, or even daily, sales targets. And you should be rewarding performance against those targets. You can help by providing daily or weekly feedback on sales performance; often this information alone is enough to maintain motivation and stimulation to achieve the goals. Make sure your goals are clearly stated in terms that will relate to the behaviour of the person in your store, then provide regular feedback on performance. Let this be the basic structure of performance in your store. From here, build on the profit improvement drive, gaining the extra motivation and performance that will make your store excellent.

Be innovative and creative

The starting point of all creativity and innovation is to identify the problems or issues that you wish to overcome. You can do this in one of two ways. First, make a list of all of the performance shortfalls in your store. A performance shortfall is any task or standard not being achieved. Second, identify any task or standard in your store that, while being satisfactorily carried out for now, would enhance the store's performance, particularly its financial performance, by being upgraded and improved. The next step is to attach priorities to all of the items on your lists. Having placed them in order of priority, select the top three to work on.

For each of the three, take a blank piece of paper and write down the problem at the top. Then, with several of your team members, have a brainstorming session to produce solutions, writing all your ideas down on the piece of paper.

Once you have identified the problems, and brainstormed ways of overcoming them, it is then a matter of reflecting quietly on the ideas you have generated, and identifying those that are practical. Do not wait for inspiration in order to become more innovative and creative. Adopt a determined, professional, systematic approach. The problems that you note might include issues such as: increasing the foot traffic through the store, improving the presentation of a particular department, or upgrading the store's appearance. The issues that arise will be specific to your store; the solutions that will emerge will also be specific. Credit for those ideas implemented must be given to the people who came up with them. This will contribute to the development in your store of a positive, creative ethic where problems are confronted quickly, attention is focused on those problems, the best ideas are selected, and then they are implemented with due discipline and effectiveness. Being more innovative and creative is merely another aspect of your management that must be worked at, instead of being put aside while you wait for inspiration. When encouraging creativity, be sure that your people think beyond the range of tradition and what has usually been done. Push the limits of the ideas. Make your staff think about the basics and the simple fundamental principles and disciplines that underlie retailing – not the techniques that you have used for the past 10 years merely because that's the way you have done things.

Don't accept no

It is easier to say sorry than to ask permission. Getting away with it simply depends on your judgment and your effectiveness at achieving results. Assume you have more authority than you have and just do it. But you had better get it right. It's conflicting advice, isn't it? How successful do you want to be? Begin slowly, identify an area, and push gently and quietly past what you think are your current limits of authority. Test the reaction when you challenge authority and take more than you feel you currently have, but test also your judgment in taking that authority. It is perhaps this second point that is more important than the first. Where in doubt, get used to contacting your boss and saying straight out, 'This is what I'm thinking of doing. What do you think about that?' Then don't accept the first negative reaction. Listen to the arguments and reasoning that are offered. Use your listening skills to explore the principles that cause the person in authority over you to react or comment the way they do. Then analyse the factors that have contributed to their judgment, be creative about overcoming them, restructure your plan to take all of this into account, and do it anyway.

When you are the owner and operator of a retail store, use an associate or a consultant or somebody within your store whom you trust to bounce ideas off. Go to conferences and question and probe and reflect, then come back and put the best ideas into practice. Always avoid complicated ideas. Keep them simple; keep them rooted in the fundamental disciplines of retailing – that is, bringing more customers into the store, merchandising and selling to them more effectively when they do come in, and maintaining the systems, disciplines and procedures that protect the store's profit potential. Stay with these fundamentals and you cannot go wrong.

Seek bottom-up profit improvement

Every week, for every department in your store, be sure to do three things. One, provide information on sales for last week against last weeks' target. Two, be sure that the sales targets for this week are clearly identified and understood. Three, ask: What will be done this week to improve this department? Every week, come up with one idea for improving the performance of every department. Sometimes it will be a merchandising idea to achieve higher levels of sales for that week – for instance, a special promotion, or a special demonstration, or a special price reduction for a period. In other weeks it might be improving the layout of the department, or altering the availability of products, or adding a new product. Large or small, the key is to have a new idea in every department every week. If your retail store is small, and there is no one in charge of a particular department, then you may have to generate the ideas yourself and gain the assistance of your staff in implementing those ideas. If your store is slightly larger, then you may be able to delegate one of your staff to spend part of their time assisting you to come up with the ideas and implementing those ideas. Whatever the nature or size of your store, the principle remains – one new idea in every department every week.

Reward people who get the results

Rewards may be financial or concerned with status. Both are important. Generate for yourself a list of rewards that you are prepared to implement. Try some of them out, then after a time replace them with others on your list. That way they don't become repetitive and boring.

Recognise, as well, that if you run a large store, your department heads are not always in a position to praise their staff who do well. For instance, a department head might praise an employee for doing something particularly well, and the employee might respond, 'Don't praise me, put it in my pay packet.' This can sometimes be difficult for the department head to manage. Where this is likely to occur, you should discuss it with your department heads, so that praise, where appropriate, is offered by yourself. A manager once removed from the individual, especially the overall manager of the store, is unlikely to receive the same sort of response. Be aware of these factors and manage them effectively. Vary the range of rewards, the ways in which people are recognised, and the status system in your store, so that the reward system remains an effective motivational tool and does not become overused, or ineffective, because of repetition.

Build a dynamic store climate

Involve staff in generating ideas

There are three problems to be overcome in involving your staff in improving your store.

The first is time: all too often there does not seem to be enough time to involve people in coming up with ideas to overcome a problem or to improve the merchandising or presentation of a department. Consequently, the manager simply rushes in and says do this or do that or do something else. Staff are not required to think, merely to carry out instructions. As a result, staff don't think, gain little satisfaction from their work, have little pride in what they do, and generally wait for the manager to generate the next set of ideas.

The second problem that discourages managers from involving staff in generating ideas could be called the 'quality' problem. That is, managers feel that they are the only ones who can come up with good-quality solutions to problems. They may take the time to ask staff, but they see the staff's ideas as inferior, so they go ahead and implement their own.

Finally, attempts to involve staff in generating ideas must be persisted with for a sufficiently long time to overcome any inherent conservatism, scepticism or downright suspicion. When you ask staff for ideas, they will probably be sceptical at first, especially if it is not the way management has conducted itself in the past – and that goes for most managers most of the time. The first step towards improving your staff's involvement in overcoming the problems they face in your store and improving its profits is for you to identify any of your behaviours that might be preventing them from putting forward their ideas. You should modify your behaviour now, thus creating the space and opportunity for your staff to generate useful suggestions.

Maintain the energy level in your store

How would you describe the energy level in your store? On a scale of one to ten, how would you estimate the entertainment value of your store? On a scale of one to ten, how much would a customer enjoy your store? Store energy is created by two main factors: the overall presentation of the store – the excitement generated by the words, the displays, the layout, the lighting, and the music; and the energy, enthusiasm and friendliness of your staff, combined with the activities of people in the store. On top of this, there will be occasional special events, such as the carpark sales for which your store is renowned throughout the city, or the mid-winter super-save week where all of the specials are truly special and people queue for the bargains.

This energy must begin with you. You must be enthusiastic on a daily basis in interacting with your people; you must be enthusiastic about generating ideas and encouraging your people to generate ideas on a weekly basis, to ensure that the department targets are met; and you must be enthusiastic on an annual basis, in coming up with ideas and events that will make your store a special place.

Smile at your customers and staff

Smile at your staff. Smile at customers. Smile at the friends of customers. Stand on the street and smile at the passers-by – nod and say hello. Smile when you feel like smiling. Smile even when you don't quite feel like smiling. Smile when you are up. Smile when you are down. Smile. Learn to separate the expression on your face from the underlying thoughts in your mind. But do so quietly, gently. Do not put on a forced, insincere smile. Learn to relax in the face of the pressure of your job.

Relax your mind, train it to be quiet and clear, so that you are aware of goals, tasks and risks, but these do not affect the expression on your face. Train your mind to hide your worries – such as whether or not that stock will arrive, or the fact that sales and cash flow are down for the week, or that you have a third of your staff away with illness – so that you are still able to smile at customers and staff alike. Your worries are yours; it is your responsibility, your job. Many of the issues cannot be delegated to other staff members, and should not be delegated unwittingly through the expression on your face or the tone of your voice. Carry your own worries.

Project warmth to your staff

You should enjoy your staff as staff, but be cautious about making your staff friends. To make your store a success, your staff must be friendly and enthusiastic towards customers, towards one another, and towards the task of creating the environment that characterises your store.

Be conscious that this requires energy from your people, and in the first instance, you must help generate that energy through the energy that you project at them. You must not be too friendly; you must maintain a sufficient emotional distance for them to know you will judge them on their work performance. But avoid allowing this emotional distance to be a cool aloofness. This will undermine the creation of a climate consistent with maximising sales.

Avoid token involvement

If you are aiming to increase the level of idea generation by your staff, then avoid token involvement – for instance, suggestion boxes. If you do implement a suggestion box, do it very thoroughly. Be sure to approach every department every week and discuss with them what ideas they are going to put into the suggestion box for that week. Publish every suggestion, no matter what it is. Aim to implement all practical, helpful suggestions. Publish what has been done and the results obtained. Go around and publicly thank those who generated the ideas. All of these activities by the manager apply equally to any other form of creative effort by your staff. Encourage every idea; encourage staff to think of new ways of doing things. Encourage and then encourage some more. Make it a deliberate policy on your part to seek ideas for the improvement of every department from every person in that department at least monthly. Set regular improvement goals. And check that they are put in place. Through this behaviour, you will encourage an attitude of constant self-improvement. Discuss this attitude, and point out that you expect your staff to adopt it as their working ethic. But be careful with your impatience, allow them their scepticism and suspicion. Proceed quietly, firmly, deliberately and directly, without rushing. Give people time to get used to the fact that you do indeed mean it, that you are sincere about the process, and that you will follow it through. Do this and watch your store benefit.

Insist on an attitude that places the customer first

Acknowledge every customer who visits your store, especially customers who are waiting to be served. Keep your promises. Always advise customers why you are unable to fulfil your obligations. Remember that there is no such thing as a good or bad customer. Say thank you. Smile. Treat every single sale as if it is the most important sale you will ever make, or certainly the most important sale you have had today. Don't burden your customers with your woes and troubles, but create an environment where they are able to unburden themselves and feel uplifted by shopping in your store.

There are no new ideas on handling customers. It is common sense. The difficulty is living it. How well do you do it, and how well do your staff do it? Talk to your staff; discuss the importance of the customer. They are bound to agree. Yet those same people will still regard the customer as an interruption when they are doing 'proper' work in the store. Quietly insist on appropriate behaviour. Quietly insist that they smile and exhibit a friendly grace that puts the customers at ease and makes them want to repeat the shopping experience.

Picture it now: one of your staff is completing a sale with a customer. It's a big sale and she is wrapping the goods and finishing the transaction with grace and friendliness. Now another customer walks into the department, your salesperson watches the newcomer out of the corner of an eye, the customer notices it, and the salesperson nods gently. Thus the customer knows that he or she has been noticed and continues browsing until the salesperson has completed the purchase. All this time the existing customer is being reassured by the salesperson's professionalism, which enables the new customer to be acknowledged without a loss of momentum in the conversation as the parcel is wrapped. The salesperson now bids a friendly farewell to the existing customer and moves across to the new customer, who is still browsing. This is demanding behaviour aimed at putting the customer first. Are scenes like this enacted in your store? How well are they enacted? And how would you improve your store's performance?

See your store from the customer's point of view

We all become accustomed to seeing what we want to see. For a retail store manager, this is simply not good enough. At least monthly, go out into the carpark, preferably with a trusted member, and discuss what you expect to achieve with your customers, how you expect them to feel, and what you expect them to see when they enter your store. Having established your objective, spend a few minutes thinking about the principles of presentation – this should be eye-catching, well organised and laid out, and entertaining as well as interesting. Once you feel you are ready to re-enter the store, then do so, looking at the store from the point of view of a customer. Take your time, move slowly and carefully examine every aspect of the store, as the customer would see it. Ask yourself : Where do the eyes travel? What do they see first? And how appealing is it?

Store blindness is a major problem that every retail manager must overcome. We must stop seeing what we want to see, begin to see objectively and clearly what the customer sees, and then improve on it. First impressions are important. Make sure that the first impression of your store is favourable. Then see to the details: Are the price tickets clear? Is the layout favourable? Can the customers reach the goods they want to reach? And so on. See the store as it really is, through a customer's eyes. Then make it more appealing for the customer.

Be creative in attracting attention

Recently a delicatessen in a supermarket increased its sale of ham products by 35 percent merely by placing a pig's head with an apple in its mouth at the centre of the delicatessen display. Why? The delicatessen was already well presented, clean and tidy, with good service. Why did the pig's head make the difference? It was simply because people noticed it; it drew their attention. People were used to rushing past the delicatessen, buying things occasionally when they were on their list or they had thought about them in advance. Now they had this pig's head staring at them with an apple in its mouth. They were amused, and as a result they bought more product. Attract people's attention. There are few or no rules. If you are in doubt, or if you are unsure as to how to go about it, then force yourself to start doing things. And then learn. Your sales will benefit.

Identify the store's faults and strengths

Take a blank piece of paper. Draw a line down the middle. On the left-hand side at the top write 'Strengths'. On the right-hand side at the top write 'Weaknesses'.

In the left-hand column list all the strengths of your store – all its competitive advantages and everything that you think makes it a good place to shop. In the right-hand column list all the weaknesses of your store – all those factors that detract from its presentation, service, or general performance. Be sure that you identify one strength for every weakness; keep your lists in balance.

Now, having created your list of strengths and weaknesses, reflect on the balance between them. What are the general themes that emerge, and where are the opportunities for improvement?

Place the weaknesses in order of priority, then develop a plan for overcoming them or dealing with them more effectively than you do now. In the first instance, try to overcome as many of the weaknesses as you can without spending money. Be creative; involve your staff and involve your customers.

Ask the staff how they would improve the store

Just as you have focused sessions with your customers about improving the store, you should hold focus sessions with your staff – either on a cross-departmental basis, where several departments are represented at once, or department by department. Be sure to set clear ground rules – for instance, the ideas are to involve no expenditure. Or set a small budget – perhaps £300 – to be spent on any one idea. Where more expenditure is involved, be willing to accept formal proposals, which will receive a formal response after being seriously considered. Make staff justify the expenditure in terms of the increase in sales and profits that will result. As you visit each department every morning, ask, 'What suggestions do you have today?' Or, in a more focused way, ask section leaders or department heads what they are going to do to improve the presentation or service or performance of their department that week. Often it is quite useful to take the department head outside, where the customer stands, get him or her to look at each aspect of that department – ticketing, presentation, staff appearance, etc. - and ask for two or three ideas for improving each aspect. Not only do managers become store blind, department heads and section leaders can become department or section blind. And it is the manager's role to help them overcome this. But always encourage ideas. And be enthusiastic and energetic about the ideas your staff generate. Your store will benefit.

Know the behaviour you expect of your staff

There are two important aspects to knowing and understanding the behaviour you expect of your staff. First, know their daily routine. Thus, when you go into a department, you should know what is going on in that department that day. Carry with you a brief summary of the routines, and check whether or not the routines are being carried out efficiently. The second aspect of knowing the behaviour you want concerns general types of behaviour, such as handling a customer or the manner in which staff are expected to relate to one another or deal with you or a supervisor.

If you are unsure of the general behaviour you require, such as dealing with a customer in a particular situation, then take a blank piece of paper and write down what behaviour you think you require, test it with a trusted member of your staff, and refine it until it creates a clear picture of what the person should do. Share it with your employees, making it clear that this is your expectation. Take time to work it through by yourself, then take more time to work it through with your staff. Work it through to the point where they too can see precisely what behaviour is necessary in order to achieve the standards that you and they believe are necessary. If you know and understand the general behaviour you seek, and if you know the routines in each department, then you can manage effectively by walking around, because you know what to look for.

Ensure that your staff know the behaviour expected of them

Identifying and establishing the behaviour you want from your people is the first critical act of leadership. The second is communicating your expectations to them. Ensure that all members of your staff know exactly what is expected of them. Ensure that they know the standards, and have access to the standards so that they can see whether or not they are meeting them. Then be sure to provide them with feedback, every week at least, on whether or not they achieved the store's goals. If you run a large store, you must of course work through your department heads. Therefore, not only do you have to check that the department heads are advising their staff, you also have to find out how effective those department heads are in communicating with their staff.

From time to time, be prepared to audit a department – that is, during a lunchtime or a morning or afternoon tea break or after work, get the department together and ask them what behaviour is expected of them, what the routines are, and how they should conduct themselves in the department. Have a series of prepared questions, if necessary, to ensure that you cover the key issues. Do this for every department, say, every six months. Be enthusiastic about service, taking care of the customer, and maintaining discipline with respect to the systems and procedures. Good merchandising and good service will build sales; good systems and procedures will ensure that the profit potential of each product is protected.

Spend time in the store

Do not be an office manager. There is always a certain amount of administration, so be organised and make sure it is done quickly and effectively. Build it into your routine, and then spend the rest of your time on the shop floor, walking around, guiding, helping, encouraging and cajoling your staff. To do this well, you must know what you are seeking and you must have communicated that clearly to your staff –

so that when you are going around you are able to say, 'Hey, remember when we talked about ...' As a guide, aim to spend 60 percent of your time in the store. If you are spending less, you need to have a very hard look at your administrative routines, delegating and reorganising and replanning and rescheduling until you can fit them into 40 percent of your time at the most. And that 40 percent should include calls by sales representatives. Be prepared to demonstrate your enthusiasm by helping out on the service desk occasionally, or by working at the checkout, or by serving in the haberdashery section, or by assisting the packers to pack. Don't do it for long – half to three-quarters of an hour is sufficient – and do it with energy and enthusiasm. Smile and chatter – not to staff, but to customers. Show your staff how you think it can be done, and where there are staff doing it better than you, be sure to praise them. Lead by being involved.

Exhibit controlled impatience with your staff when necessary

People can be exasperating. But, as a leader, you must manage your frustration and exasperation and not let your ill humour affect the relationship between you and your staff. That is not to say you cannot get angry. If you are, you should display it, but in a controlled way. Nor is there any point in saying quietly and softly, 'You are making me angry.' If you are angry, you must say so with controlled intensity and purpose. Be assertive with staff who are talking too long or taking too long over a particular simple task. Don't necessarily be overbearing about it; make it easy by saying things like, 'I hope you're not going to be much longer at that, because it shouldn't take that long really.' You have made the point, they know you have made the point, they know they are in the wrong, and you have carried out your leadership role effectively.

Improve recruitment

When recruiting, have a clear idea of what you want

If you are looking for a shop assistant, accounts clerk, or branch manager, you probably have a good understanding of the nature of the job. However, you need to go beyond this and gain insight into the essence of the job as you expect it to be carried out. For instance, you may be recruiting an invoice and accounts clerk in your store, and the list of duties may be straightforward and appropriate. However, the essence of the job is to cope with the multitude of tasks that have to be done in any one day, to impose order on a paper flow of considerable proportions, and to handle queries from other staff, yourself, suppliers, and people seeking credit. The essence of the job is not whether somebody can in fact function efficiently as an accounts clerk, but whether that person can effectively operate what amounts to a sole charge office – whether he or she has the maturity to stay calm and collected and effective despite the pressure resulting from endless queries and a never-ending flow of paper.

In a similar way, shop assistants in a supermarket and a sports goods store may appear on paper to have a very similar set of tasks. However, the essence of their jobs is quite different. Generally speaking, the supermarket assistant serves customers in a relatively passive manner, though, where appropriate, he or she encourages customers to make add-on purchases. The shop assistant in a sports goods store, on the other hand, should be anything but passive, approaching customers, soliciting interest, enquiring about customers' needs, providing product guidelines that meet those needs, overcoming objections, and closing the sale. It is a much more intense selling situation.

These examples are intended merely to make a point. What is the essence of the job in your store for which you are recruiting? Take a little more time to think about the job as it really is, and use this insight to guide your search for an appropriate and suitably qualified candidate.

Prepare for the recruitment interview

First, you must ensure that you fully understand the job and its essence. The next stage is to ask what qualifications are needed, or what background experience is needed, to carry out this job successfully?

Draw up a qualification specification.

* What past experience should the person have?
* What sort of knowledge should they have?
* Do they need any formal qualifications?
* What sort of courses should they have attended?
* How many years' experience should they have and in what fields?

Be sure that your list is realistic; do not make it a wish list. Be sure that it bears some relationship to the candidates you are likely to attract with the advertisements and search method you intend to use. Having established the background, experience and qualifications of the person, what sort of person do you want? What should be their key personal attributes? And how should they exhibit that in behaviour? For instance, if you expect to recruit a good salesperson, candidates should sell you themselves.

You should be testing them from your very first interaction with them. They should begin selling themselves when they first telephone to arrange an interview. Or, if they send a resumé, it should sell you the benefits of employing them.

In a similar way, when recruiting clerical staff, look for neatness and precision, and if looking for a person to handle a high-pressure position, then look for the poise and quiet good sense that come with maturity.

Prepare for the interview. Understand the essence of the job, know the qualifications, background and experience that are necessary, and have a reasonable idea of the sort of person, the type of personality, you seek. And think about how these attributes should be exhibited in an interview. If you do this, you will know the person when you encounter him or her.

Be creative in your search for job candidates

Quite often, the problem is not knowing good candidates when you meet them, but getting them to apply in the first place. Three pieces of advice, if thoroughly applied, will assist your search.

- First, be sure that the income package you are offering is competitive – not just competitive within your industry, but competitive generally – in order to attract good people.

- Second, be sure that your advertisements are vigorous, using energetic imagery without appearing insincere or shallow.

- Third, be creative in where and how you seek applicants. Use all the means at your disposal to ensure a steady stream of good people applying for positions in your store.

Before beginning a recruitment campaign, think about all the possible ways of obtaining candidates. These could include using a consultancy, advertising directly in newspapers, word of mouth among staff members or your own friends and family, placing a notice in the store, or arranging an announcement on the local radio station. Finally, be persistent. Seeking candidates for jobs is rather like fishing; the pool is large and your hook is relatively small.

Be prepared to confront people

Your responsibility is to get the best people you can and to be sure that they can do what they say they can do. To get the best people, you need to sell them the benefits of your organisation and enthuse them about working for you. To be sure that they can do what they say they can do, you need to confront them, test them thoroughly on any skills they say they have, and check their references.

There is clearly conflict between selling them the job and checking them out. And the way in which you resolve this conflict will determine your success at getting the best qualified and most appropriate employees.

It is often said that you should not sell someone a job you are offering, and this is true if you have a long enough list of well-qualified candidates. At that point, you can afford to be more detached. However, when you are competing for candidates, and the candidates know that they have other job openings available to them, then you have little or no choice. Selling the job can be done while you give a basic description of it to the candidate. Always take the extra step of pointing out the benefits of the job to them – how they will be involved with it, the satisfaction that will result from doing the job well, and other benefits offered by the company (i.e. not just the financial benefits, but the personal and social benefits that come from working in your tight close-knit team). If, at any point, you feel that the candidate is interviewing you, and does have other job opportunities in mind, then you should perhaps be a little more detached and cool, making clear the benefits of working for you and your team. And leave it at that. Allow the candidate to make up his or her own mind.

Regardless of how hard you may be selling the job to the candidate, be sure that you test the skills and abilities that the candidate claims to have. For instance, specific skills such as typing, using a cash register, or general clerical duties should be tested as far as possible. At the very least, ask candidates to describe exactly and succinctly to you what they would do under certain circumstances. And look for some congruence – for example, if you are recruiting a salesperson, expect them to sell to you. If they do not, confront them and ask them why they are not selling to you as you would have expected. If you are seeking poise and maturity, ask direct, partially irrelevant questions and then assess their response and the poise of their response. For example, ask: 'Are you religious?' or 'You don't seem to be very sociable; would you care to comment on that?' Or look for the one aspect in their application that requires scrutiny. For instance, if they have had several jobs over a short period of time, refer to this directly and ask them to explain themselves. Listen to their answers, but also watch the poise with which they manage themselves. This will often tell you more than the answers themselves. Look for the quiet assurance, the sincerity, and the directness that sit comfortably with your instincts. After an interview, a candidate for one of your jobs should feel interviewed. If the candidate does not, then you are doing yourself a disservice.

If in doubt, delay

Don't be tempted to give somebody a job merely because you need somebody in that job. You may find, later, that you simply recruited a bigger problem than you had when you had no one in the job in the first place. And if you have interviewed a number of people, none of whom are quite adequate, don't be tempted to select the best candidate if the overall standard was low. If in doubt, delay. Rerun the advertisement; take your time. It is your business and your profits.

Seek a second opinion

When interviewing for junior jobs in your store, or perhaps opening a new store and having to see a lot of candidates, it often pays to have one person doing the interviewing and another merely watching. Then you can compare notes afterwards on the people you have seen. This way you get a more balanced view of your candidates and probably better selection. If you must interview on your own, and the job is more senior, then always seek a second opinion, even if it's from one of your trusted staff who will have to work with the individual. If the job is a very senior job in your organisation, there should be an even more intensive selection process. There should be at least two interviews by yourself, another interview by a second person, and possibly even personality profiles put together by a consultant. Personality profiles, and psychological tests generally, must be treated with caution, but they do assist the decision-making process. In summary, interview with more vigour and directness. Be prepared to assess openly and directly. At the same time, be prepared to sell the job to good candidates.

Check references

A very small minority of candidates will quite happily tell blatant lies about their work experience. The vast majority, however, will merely ensure that the words they use paint a favourable picture of themselves with respect to their previous experience.

Always check references.

Make new staff feel welcome

Adopt a simple standard process for settling any new staff into your store. One such process might be as follows:

- Have a clear-cut and specific job description, so they know what to do on the first day.

- Be sure that when they arrive, all the necessary administrative preparation has been done – that accounts know about them and have their tax forms ready, that any other forms are ready, and so on.

- Be sure to introduce them immediately to the key people they are going to be working with. If it is a large store, put their photograph and a brief statement on the notice board. It is not necessarily a good idea to rush around a large store trying to introduce them to everybody on the first day. Get them settled in first, introduce them to the key people they are going to be working with immediately, and appoint a buddy to help them settle into the routines of the store. Then, perhaps two or three weeks later, go around and make sure they have been introduced to other store staff.

- Check that they understand the basic routines – morning and afternoon teas, where to find the toilets, the routine for arrival and departure, what to do in case of a fire drill, and where to go to ask for information should they need it. They will not necessarily be comfortable about approaching you, as manager, for information, so ensure that somebody else is available, such as a buddy or a supervisor, or a personnel manager if you have one. Make new staff feel welcome.

Train frequently

Use training to maintain positive attitudes and focus. Be sure that any new people, and the rest of your staff, are trained in the basic routines of the store, have the necessary sales skills befitting their job, and have the necessary product knowledge. If people are supervisors, make sure that they have the necessary supervisory and leadership training. Administration, sales and product training should be carried out as an ongoing function of your branch or department meetings. It should be done by you, and also by your department heads at their own meetings. Of course, if you are expecting your department heads to conduct training in this way, you must train them to be able to conduct the training. If you build their confidence in what they are doing, they are more likely to do it more often and more effectively.

Train more often. Encourage your supervisory staff to train more often. And encourage all the staff in your store to train one another using the expertise each of them has. If somebody has particularly detailed knowledge about an administrative system, or a particular product line, use them to train the rest of the staff. Give them that status, and encourage all staff to gain some particular area of expertise that they can subsequently pass on to the rest of the staff.

Target all training by asking people what they are going to do differently as a result of their training, what additional results they will achieve, and what goals they will realise. This ensures that your training pays for itself.

Set clear standards and live them yourself

Tell people what is expected of them

Retailing, like all business, depends on an aggressive attitude towards generating ideas. And, of course, lots of energy. It is often argued that a good manager should not be aggressive.

However, it is essential that a manager, especially an owner-manager, be aggressive. This does not mean that you should be belligerent and unpleasantly argumentative, but that you should be aggressive with planning and thinking, be aggressive with the market, but always be gracious with people. In particular, you must be aggressive, firm and determined about the standards you set for your team. The standards flow from the manager. And they depend, first and foremost, on the manager's own standards. Setting and achieving high standards is important in all businesses, but it is the very essence of success in retailing. A retailer is 'on show'. Retail customers are the essential participants in the show. It follows that the presentation must always be up to standard if the show is to gain the essential word-of-mouth support. Not for the retailer the luxury of dirty and untidy premises so often encountered among small (and sometimes large) manufacturers.

As an aside, it is worth noting that the cleanliness aboard an American naval vessel is the responsibility of the executive officer (the ship's number two). The relationship between cleanliness, morale and operational standards is seen to be of such importance that it is the USN commander who checks that the loos are clean. Begin setting the standards and making it clear to people what you expect of them by setting higher standards for yourself.

Pick up pieces of paper

How often do you, as manager, rush around the store being busy while continually stepping over price tickets lying on the carpet, or pieces of string that dropped off the serving counter, or discarded wrapping paper? How often do you talk to your staff about keeping the store tidy, keeping the shelves tidy, picking up rubbish? One of the keys to establishing excellent attitudes in your store is to exhibit those attitudes in your behaviour. Begin today – resolve to pick up those bits of rubbish, to take the time to tidy the shelf or straighten the price ticket. Begin to see every detail of your store, to notice any untidiness, to make small moves yourself to correct it, and to delegate the task to others where the amount of effort required is beyond that which you can offer there and then. Set the standard being busy, but not too busy to do the small corrective tasks that can be done while you are moving through the store on your normal routines. By doing this, you will encourage all your staff to do the same.

Provide the focus and direction

Aggression, to be effective, demands an appropriate focus. Four key success factors for retailing are:

1   identifying your market
2   offering appropriate services

3   setting appropriate store standards
4   having a framework of store routines as the backbone of your retail operation.

Who are your customers? What do they buy? And how can they be contacted? If, for example, your market is the local community, then advertise in the local paper, sponsor the local school fair, belong to local clubs, and get to know people. If your market is the well dressed and well off, then cater to their attitudes, values and tastes. So who are you selling to? Target your efforts at them. The service has to be consistent with your market.

What does it feel like to come into your store? Is it a good shopping experience? Do your staff smile? Are they well informed on the products? Is their manner brisk, businesslike, but also friendly? Generate the energy in your people. Servicing the public can be hard. It takes energy to project towards the customer. Adopt approving behaviours and cheerleading to help your people maintain their energy.

In addition, your store must be organised appropriately for the type of market that you are servicing. If you are offering a warehouse, then the goods have to be arranged appropriately: ready access around the aisles, good signs to direct people to products, and adequate checkouts. On the other hand, if your shop offers individualised service, then there must be adequate staff numbers to cope with the customers, and they must be capable of providing the level of service appropriate for the store and its pricing structure.

Not all goods will necessarily be on display, for example, in a shoe store; while the style may be on display, the particular size a customer is seeking may not be. Be sure that your people understand the philosophy underlying your store and that their service matches that philosophy. Set clear store standards, then ensure that the staff know those standards and can deliver them.

- **Housekeeping standards** cover the shop front, the trading area, offices, amenities, and storerooms.

- **Service standards** cover cash registers, checkouts, clear aisles, the mode of sale, layby arrangements, the customer service desk, and cheque and credit card systems.

- **Stock control standards** cover damaged stock, markdowns, ordering out-of-stocks, stock rotation, and shelf filling.

- **Presentation and merchandising standards** cover promotion plans eye appeal, dump tables, ticketing, advertisement tie-ups, window displays, discount displays, and product appeal.

- **Selling standards** cover competitive pricing, the use of public address systems, promoting departments, 'red-light' specials, sales reviews, staff sale skills and staff motivation.

And then there are key systems:

- records of key-holders
- closing and opening duties
- burglar alarms
- what to do in the event of shoplifting
- storeroom security
- goods-in and goods-out procedures
- cash security and cash-handling controls
- authorising invoices and their payment
- authorising stock purchases
- fire extinguishers, fire drills and precautions
- emergency phone numbers
- procedures for dealing with damaged goods and goods returned.

Finally, there are the manager's daily diaries, staff and department reviews, routines cards, expense controls and wages and salaries.

Staff should know what is expected from them in each case; they should know what to do and the standard required. Store routines are essential. It is the store routines that protect the profit potential of the store. For instances, inadequate goods-in procedures may well result in invoices being paid for goods that were not received. This can significantly erode the profits of the store.

Below is a checklist to assist you to identify the standards necessary. It will pay to tick alongside the items you feel you could improve in your store, or items that need to be checked regularly.

Store housekeeping

Cleaners ☐
Shop front ☐
Trading area ☐
Offices ☐
Amenities ☐
Storerooms and loading bay ☐

Service

Cash registers ☐
Checkout ☐
Clear aisles ☐
Mode of sale ☐
Layby arrangements ☐
Customer service desk ☐
Cheque and credit card systems ☐

Stock Control

Stockholding ☐
Stockturn ☐
Damaged stock ☐
Markdowns ☐
Ordering out-of-stocks ☐
Stock rotation ☐
Stockroom ☐
Shelf-filling ☐
Scales checked ☐

Presentation and Merchandising

Promotion plans ☐

Eye appeal ☐
Dump tables ☐
Ticketing ☐
Advertisement tie-ups ☐
Window displays ☐
Pavement boards ☐
Department signs ☐
Discount displays ☐
Product appeal ☐
Product displays ☐

Selling
Competitive pricing ☐
Use of public address system ☐
Promoting departments ☐
'Red-light' specials ☐
Sales reviews ☐
Staff sales skills ☐
Staff product knowledge ☐
Staff motivation ☐

Systems
Records of key-holders ☐
Closing duties ☐
Opening duties ☐
Burglar alarms ☐
Storeroom security ☐
Goods-in procedures ☐
Goods-out procedures ☐
Checking packing slips ☐
Pricing procedures ☐
Damaged and returned goods procedures ☐
Staff parcels procedures ☐
Cash-handling controls ☐
Cash security ☐
Authorising invoices ☐

Payment of invoices ☐
Authorisation of stock purchases ☐
Extensions of invoices ☐
Fire extinguishers checked ☐
Fire drills and staff talks on fire precautions ☐
Emergency phone numbers clearly displayed ☐
Manager's daily diary ☐
Staff and department reviews ☐
Routine cards ☐
Expense controls ☐
Wages and staff scheduling ☐

Shoplifting
Staff know procedure ☐
Security controls ☐
Store detectives ☐
Staff observant ☐

Provide the focus for the staff in your store. Your store's performance will benefit.

Be consistent with the standards

Once you are convinced that the major issues in your store are under control, then you should take each of the key areas above in turn and raise the standard you expect. For example, if you are a local retailer, expect your staff to know the homes of your regular customers and to become involved in the community, and seek creative ways of rewarding them as the sales increase. Concentrate your efforts on each of the key areas for two months, without allowing any slip in the other standards. Then, once all the key areas have been addressed, begin again and repeat the process. Keep repeating to your people the key issues of market, service, standards and routines, market, service, standards and routines ... Repeat it until it almost becomes boring. Talk to them about each of those areas. Make these factors the values that pervade the behaviour in your store. Get them to understand why these issues are important. Do this and you indeed will have an excellent store.

Follow up

It is essential to follow up. Have a routine of checking aspects of your store every day. What are the key things that need to be checked? Check them. Ensure that your staff understand this routine and that the things you are to check have in fact been effectively actioned. In establishing this routine, be sure that you do not ignore other important performance areas. To do this and to do it well, you must know your store. You must understand your customers and what they seek, you must know the standard you require – only by knowing these things thoroughly can you possibly walk around your store and ensure that standards are being met.

Select one or two of the ideas here to apply each quarter and watch your store flourish.

INDEX

For a complete list of Management Books 2000 titles,
visit our web-site at http://www.mb2000.com

Retail Store Leadership

 LEARNING SUPPORT SERVICES

Please return
on or before
the last date
stamped below

 City College
NORWICH

A FINE WILL BE CHARGED FOR OVERDUE ITEMS